Learn Greek in 25 Years

A crash course
for the linguistically challenged

Brian Church

Athens News

1st edition   1999
Reprinted   2000
2nd reprint 2002
3rd reprint 2004
4th reprint 2006

ISBN 960-86395-1-4

Printed and bound in Athens,
Greece by Psyllidis Graphic Arts S.A.
Pre-press by Multimedia S.A.

To my father, David C. Church,
who taught me to laugh, worry and write

and Cus *(Djordje Crncevic), Jude, Lela, John Perikos and the Chios Gum Mastic Growers Association, the very special Evi Andrikopoulou, Derek Gatopoulos, Tania Kollias, Alekos 'No Women' Name Withheld Upon Request, Tania 'Trouble' Bozaninou, Miss Paris Agiomamitis, Daniela and all Costa Ricans everywhere, Nikoletta Papadimitriou, Alexis Yiannas, Stella Sevastopoulou, Dr Anthony Pigram, Helen Papadakou, Evi Vogli, Uncle Bernard, Aunty Margaret, Paul, Dailwen, Nathanael and Bethany, Natassa Vassilaki, George Gilson, Evgenia Georgopoulou, Mum, Sophia Sofikitis, fellow Cretan Dr Manolis Polentas PhD, Olga Malea, Sophia 'No plans' Bacoula, Sophia and Samantha Glass, the 1998 Paraguayan World Cup football squad (you tried your best), Marcus Gibson, Stefanos and Andreas, my courageous teacher and Macedonian friend Dora Papaioannou, Dr Mark Pickett, Paula Mence, Athens News page layout crew - Cleo, Nektarios, Yiannis, Nikos and Katerina, Mr Giampaolo Gandolfo whose support from afar has meant more than he will ever know, Lambis Sideris, Charles 'The biggest problem in journalism today is financial illiteracy' Kotsonis, Demetris Nellas, chess, juggling and unicycling partner Nicholas Paphitis, George Kolyvas, the computing gods upstairs led by Dimitris 'Excellence is the enemy of Good' Tsambouris (or should that be the other way round?), Daphne Kasriel, Diane Shugart, Costas Pipilios, Mrs Daisy 'Don't mind if I do' Williams, Uncle Trevor, Aunty Carol, Kim, Gary and Darren, Iris from Plaka, everyone in the 5th floor cafe (Andreas, Christos, Mitsos, Dionysis, Dimitris, Agathocles, Nikos and Spyros), nieces Sarah, Annette, Siobhan, Rachel & Lorea and nephews Luke & Joseba, Daisy 'Strictly No Ice' Williams, Shibly Nabhan, Patricia (Patou) Ferrari, all security guards at 3 Christou Lada, Annika Zacharias, Tina Zafiri, June Field, Maria 'Thank you for coming back' Paravantes, Helen 'Doc' Iatrou, Nikos Konstandaras, Philip Pangalos, Thomas Papapaschalis & Mary ('CP') Kalikas, Alexia Amvrazi, Theophilos 'School Bus' Argitis, Rob, Maria 'Hold my calls' Angelopoulou, Nikos 'Foxy' Alepous, Tatiana Capodistria, Eddie Brannigan, J.C. Hadoulis, Dinos Mitsis, George Dillon Slater, Mary Sinanidis, Helena Economidou, Maria from Chios, Tina Katsounakis, Dina Pinos, Christine Pirovolakis, Maria from Chios again, Mariane Georgopoulos, June Prentice and all past members of Hams (Hellenic Amateur Musical Society, sorry for calling it the musical wing of Hamas), Takis Sfalagakos, Louis Economopoulos, Helen Wynne, Greg Ray, Nick Bakos, Elsie Tsouti, one more time for Maria from Chios, Duncan Skinner, John Comninos, Yiannis Yiannakopoulos, Megaklis, Argyro Karageorgiou, Uncle Stewart, Aunty Gladys, Sharon and Alistair, Mr A (Nikiforos Antonopoulos), my favourite sister-in-law Begona Iturbe and three great brothers-in-law - Paul Williams, Dave Janes and Dr Kevin Bowers, Nikos 'Time is on our side' Sazaklis, Evelyn Spiekerman von Wiesenburg (sic), George the Cheerful, Maria from Chios' sister Lilly, Michalis Arvanitopoulos, any driver of the 126 Athens-Paleo Faliro bus, Fofi Katsibra and the Posidonia 98 team, Yolanda Valassopoulou, Kathy Tzilivakis, Angelika 'Life is what you make of it' Timms, Carla Day, Allan Alt+Tab Wilson, Emi Zervas and her father, Thanasis Vasiliadis, Bina, Dr R.U. Yakovee, Ilias Katsanis, William 'Snoop' Papatassos, Daisy 'Fill it up' Williams, Ylva Wigh, Athina Flamboura (I want that coffee), Uncle Colin, Aurelia and Rosina, Cassandra Evans, Sissy (είμαστε;), Vlasia Myari, diplomatic correspondent Andrew Leech, Daisy 'Call that a glass?' Williams, Nigel Lowry, Mr Costas, Pat, Debbie, Mike and Sue, Yiannis Donekian, Natasha Giannoussi, Elinda Labropoulou, Daniel Howden, Marilena Vandorou, everyone at the Haratzas School in Kifissia, Peter Heilmann, John Rodgers, E.S.Kingdom and the Right Reverend Jimmy Johnson*

all of whom, except Uncle Stewart, promised to buy this book if I dedicated it to them

Contents

Acknowledgements

Learn Greek in 25 Years could never have started life, yet alone withered, without the unwanted help of an amazingly diverse collection of homegrown lunatics at the *Athens News*. And to this very day, the same journalists, often naked, continue to answer my every question about their remarkable language with suggestions, comments and other obscenities.

One colleague, a fully clothed Dinos Mitsis, has patiently read, corrected and given advice since I began teaching readers Greek in January 1997. More than anyone else, he represents Greece in my eyes, overflowing with fun, fire and (fully forgivable) faults. If I ask him how to spell a 35-letter Greek word, he always responds: 'As it sounds, Brian, as it sounds.'

Rena Karakatsani, a professional translator, looked over this book's manuscript, making hundreds of invaluable improvements. Of course, all mistakes - grammatical, factual and being born English - are mine. Allan Wilson, a distinguished linguist who speaks Hebrew, Greek, German and English, was consulted at various stages and had the audacity to point out several errors. Praise be also to Maria Paravantes.

Most dictionaries define a Greek as 'someone who physically threatens you with his right hand whilst filling up your glass with his left'. And far too many Greek friends, and indeed strangers from all nations (led by Scotland), have poured me another to name them all. The Gatopoulos clan have looked after me like a sister and son ever since I came to live in Athens seven years ago.

The centimetre-challenged Paris Agiomamitis, who stares at the ceiling like we normals look at the sun, has made me laugh at work almost every day.

Ginormous thanks must go to *Athens News* editor Romolo Gandolfo for being the driving force behind this book.

Producing a book, however small, is a horrible burden for

anyone to bear and I have to thank Constanza Miliou and, especially, Irene Pitoura for their intrepid work.

For the record, the title of my weekly column, and hence this book, was inspired by Hara Garoufalia-Middle's *Greek in a Week*. It was from this somewhat optimistic tome that I first learnt:

Το δωμάτιό μου έπιασε φωτιά
My (hotel) room is on fire

I very much hope readers find this book just as helpful.

Brian Church
Χαϊ Γουίκομ, February 1999

As far as I know, no one, including myself, has learnt any Greek through reading this book. I suspect this might be its biggest selling point. I've not changed anything (it's too hot) and there's still the 'sad ending' which attracted so much attention.

Death is the main problem with a course of such longevity and, regrettably, two of the people mentioned in the original dedication have indeed died. A couple more are pretty close. I'll update you next time.

Brian Church
Χαϊ Γουίκομ, August 2002

Good news. Nobody's died.

Brian Church
Χαϊ Γουίκομ, June 2004

Bad news. Daisy's gone.

Brian Church
Χαϊ Γουίκομ, June 2006

12

Introduction

According to one study, around 98% of Greek words are food-related. There's a famous proverb: 'You can lead Costas to a taverna but you can't make him leave it.' This love of food, combined with the national obsession for asking people how much they paid for anything, means that visiting dignitaries are forever having to listen to the popular ballad, *How much is that sausage in the window?*

The food really is nice, and the people even nicer, but that's not why I came. Deeply in love and equally deeply in debt, I arrived in 1992 with one misguided intention: To make love *in Greek* to a painfully beautiful Cretan. It was not to be *(I Do, She Doesn't* - Page 95) and I subsequently moved house four times in 16 months *(Giving directions & the art of lying - Lesson 11).*

At this point I realised that I needed a little bit of Greek in order to survive each day *(Getting on the bus - Lesson 4, Getting off the bus - Lesson 5),* to swear at taxi drivers *(Block your ears Homer! - Lesson 22)* and to apologise to friends the morning after *('If the firemen find a cigarette lighter...' - Lesson 14).* Watching me learn Greek would also help any new woman in my life *(Asking someone out - Lesson 6)* put her problems in perspective.

The critics said this course was far too ambitious. No one, in a mere 25 years, could possibly glean even a superficial understanding of Greek, not least the language's unrivalled grammatical tapestry *(The - Lesson 25),* magnificently woven under the eternal cultural sun of Ancient Greece *(Didactic Aeschylus and flutterings of the semi-soul - Lesson 9).* But at least - I'm only joking, there ain't no such lesson baby - we can try. Bear in mind I'm thicker than most of you when it comes to learning basic things in Greek *(Answering the phone - Lesson 7, Telling the time (and other miracles) - Lesson 9, Days of the week - Lesson 24).* My Greek, by the way, has shot up from shockingly abysmal to impressively dreadful since starting this column. Perhaps we should all write one?

In keeping with the book's desire to serve, no transliteration guide for pronouncing Greek words is given, though the second lesson *(Why does the 'r' look like a 'p', mummy?)* will make up for the first *(Welcome to Greek! You haven't a chance)*. There is a little stab at the alphabet on Page 91 but to be honest I wouldn't bother. Most nouns in the lessons have been put in the nominative form for your convenience. You don't know what this means, I don't know what this means but I was told to put it in, alright?

Do be put off by the huge vocabulary *(100 verbs - Lesson 12, O happy day! - Lesson 15, Useful phrases - Lesson 20)*. Actually, it can be fun looking up a word *(Sweet, succulent and just asking for it - Lesson 10)* and trying to read children's stories in another language *(Once upon a time... - Lesson 19)*. Readers currently on strong medication might well enjoy Lesson 18 *(An army of lips: How to remember Greek words)*.

My teaching philosophy is based on distance learning: The further you get from a subject, the more likely you are to conquer it. In my experience, only Cypriots, Greeks and Basques find Greek relatively easy to learn, especially Basques, although English *(George Bernard So - Lesson 16)*, American *(It's all boondocks to me - Lesson 23)* and Spanish *(Greek-Spanish - Lesson 13)* students will stumble across much they would easily recognise if they weren't English, American or Spanish.

Why make such an effort to learn Greek? At the very least it can help us enjoy our stay in Greece so much more, including outdoor chess *(Bishop takes Aunty Gladys - Lesson 21)*, discussing current affairs *(Oh dear, politics - Lesson 8)* and being in good company *(When your toilet overflows: Meeting neighbours for the first time - Lesson 3*, the original described by a friend's elderly aunt as the most disgusting article she had ever read).

If you don't have any of these pleasures in your life, there's always the Bible *(Lesson 17)*. Does God speak Greek? I doubt it.

LESSON 1

Welcome to Greek!
You haven't a chance

Once upon a time *(μια φορά κι έναν καιρό)*, whilst the jury was still deliberating, my brother flew to Spain *(Ισπανία)* and I hurried off to Greece *(Ελλάδα)*. At Madrid Airport he was asked for his *pasaporte* (see Lesson 13). At Athens Airport they wanted to see my *διαβατήριο*. Guess who learnt the local lingo first?

And if you guessed wrongly, *συγχαρητήρια* (congratulations), you've stolen the right book.

Although finding your luggage at Athens Airport often takes much longer, learning Greek is by far the single most important step to settling down in Greece. It'll also save you a lot of stress. Anyone who's ever fallen in love with a Greek god/goddess will recognise the following situation: You've flown 5,000 kilometres for your first-ever meeting with the prospective in-laws and a few close relatives. Despite practising all week, you suddenly forget the polite and plural form of *γεια σου* (hello/goodbye, pronounced 'ya sue', the 'ya' as in yak or yukelele spelt wrongly) as you walk into the crowded stadium. What do you do?

1) Greet everyone individually and informally with *γεια σου, γεια σου, γεια σου, γεια σου, γεια σου*, is that real?, *γεια σου, γεια σου*

2) Walk away

3) Use another phrase you learnt earlier: *Νομίζω ότι η Ελλάδα θα εκπληρώσει τα κριτήρια για το EMU* (I think Greece will meet the European Monetary Union criteria)

This short-term course is specially designed for those who answered 1 or 3. Readers who opted for 4 will find it particularly useful. *Σιγά-σιγά* (slowly-slowly), by the year 2024 you will remember to use *γεια σου* when addressing a child or a friend who is alone. *Γεια σας* (pronounced 'ya sas') is for greeting two or more people - readers who have only one friend can skip this bit - someone you don't know very well and anyone who is much older, bigger, richer or more successful than yourself. I use it quite a lot.

To succeed on this course, you must commit yourself to learning at least one word (preferably Greek) every day. This requires real sacrifice and support from your family. You think I'm joking but I'm not. Ask foreigners who have lived in Greece all their lives but don't speak any Greek. Or ask me. I've been here many years yet still have problems with my own five-letter name, Brian, which in Greek is the similar-looking, seven-character *Μπράιαν*. When I got to Athens, my first decision was to look for any job going. The second was to never sign a petition.

A word a day for a quarter of a century works out at a grand vocabulary of 9,131 which is more than enough to talk confidently to a Cretan farmer for some seven seconds and much more if you are the one listening.

In this lesson we have a difficult word to learn: *Γάτα* (cat), pronounced GA-ta. If you changed the g to c and got rid of the last a, you'd end up with...cat! Random reordering and obliteration of letters is just one of the many helpful tricks for learning this language. The good news is that almost 22% of English words have a Greek root. The bad news is that 74% of such words have subtly changed their meaning over the course of time. For example, 'book lover' in Greek now means 'car thief' in English.

You're probably already feeling totally baffled and tempted to throw in the *πετσέτα*. What a good idea! It's not just the language. Part of the exciting challenge of Greece is its total unpredictability. A competition to find a song summing up the country's delightful way of life was won by Manfred Mann's *Do Wah Diddy Diddy*

Dum Diddy Do. The Beatles' *I Am The Walrus* came a close second. True, you will never be bored. There is a liberating (and humane) attitude to life, offering freedom from rules and restrictions. If we all had nine lives to live, the first would surely be in Greece, followed by prolonged rest in eight English-speaking nations.

Should you regrettably decide to persevere with Greek, my ambition at the end of our 25 years together is to lead a demonstration through Constitution Square *(Πλατεία Συντάγματος)*, the heart of Athens better known as plain and simple Syntagma, with the stress on 'Sin'. I can see myself on television *(τηλεόραση)*, shouting out the verb bits for you lot to repeat: *Γράφω!* (I write!), *γράφεις!* (you write!), *γράφει!* (he/she/it writes!)...

And we could certainly march for a long time since Greek is gloriously rich, judging by the number of words an average native speaker uses in day-to-day conversation. These core vocabularies naturally vary from tongue to tongue, including English (6), French (516) and Greek (456,778).

This means that, in theory, it is 76,129.666 times as difficult to learn Greek as it is to pick up English. In practice, of course, everyone knows that Greek is much, much harder than that. You haven't a chance.

WORDS I REALLY MUST TRY TO LEARN

η γάτα	cat
γεια σου	hello (informal, singular)
γεια σας	hello (formal, plural)
το διαβατήριο	passport
σιγά-σιγά	slowly-slowly
γράφω	to write
Ελλάδα	Greece
συγχαρητήρια	congratulations
το Σύνταγμα	the Constitution
ο κοκοφοίνικας	cocopalm

LESSON 2

Why does the 'r' look like a 'p', mummy?

Let's be fair. The only thing wrong with the Greek alphabet is that it's not in alphabetical order. And it's in Greek.

The alphabet *(αλφάβητο)* probably puts more people off learning Greek than anything else. Nor is it good for your eyes. Without my glasses *(γυαλιά)* I can see reasonably well. With my super-powerful spectacles I'm almost blind *(τυφλός)*. And all because at the local optician's I had trouble reading the Greek letters chart.

Trying to work out why the sixth letter Z is so obviously in the wrong place is not our only problem. The Greek R (Ρ/ρ) is the world's P, the H is not H and Υ/υ neither Y nor u while the small ν is naturally n. And ω is not w but o - and so on.

That's not all. Concerning correct pronunciation, there are some utterances which, no matter how hard you try, can't be given an equivalent sound in English, such as when you spill a Greek's drink or wake him up early.

Letters are the only instance in which I recommend *not* asking Greek friends for help - listen to them speak instead. As soon as you get into the quagmire of pronunciation, forget it. Your life is over. Nor do the teach yourself Greek books, which give long lists of complicated rules, help at all. They miss the point. If we were capable of remembering these silly rules, we wouldn't be reading the silly book in the silly first place. The great strength of *Learn*

Greek in 25 Years is that, due to time pressure, it simplistically simplifies the simply unsimplifiable. Only I have acquired the mansions of ignorance needed to divide the Greek alphabet of 24 letters into three groups. I have entitled these thus:

Piece of cake

α ε ζ κ λ μ ν ο π σ/ς τ φ ω

Slightly awkward

β δ η θ ι ρ υ χ

Atrocious

γ ξ ψ

In my opinion - and since this is my book, my opinion counts for quite a lot and certainly far more than yours - 13 letters are easy: A/α (cat - I don't mean for you to say cat every time you see this letter, rather that the letter α is pronounced as in cat and can we get on with the other letters please?), E/ε (as in bet) and Z/ζ, K/κ, Λ/λ, M/μ, N/ν, Π/π, Σ/σ, T/τ and Φ/φ which are not really any different from z, k, l, m, n, p, s, t and f in English. The small σ changes into ς if it's at the end of a word. Why? Because it does. There are two o's - O/o (omikron) and Ω/ω (omega) - both spoken like the o in *hymenopterous* or *of*.

As for the awkwardish letters, B/β is actually V, so that lovely Greek word *βολικός* (comfortable/easy-going) comes out as voli-KOS. Δ/δ is the th in then, while H/η, I/ι, Y/υ and the dipthongs ει and οι are all the same - the e in feet. In response to reader interest, we'll come back to dipthongs in 2012 (if you're really keen see Page 91) but note that they severely complicate looking up words in dictionaries. What you hear could be spelt six or seven different ways. The popular English mnemonic, *i before e except after c,* has the Greek equivalent of *Use ita (η) rather than iota (ι) except when it's ipsilon (υ) or epsilon & iota (ει) or omikron & iota (οι) or sigma (σ) or Friday.*

Θ/θ is th from thick. X/χ is either h as in helicopter *(χαίρετε!* -

hello!) or the ch in loch (ζάχαρη - sugar). I can hear my Greek friends tutting away.

The letter ρω (P/ρ) is a real rotter, being the English r and not p. Try memorising Greek words you know are pronounced in English with an r, for example ρεβόλβερ (revolver) and ρεπόρτερ (reporter). Personally I prefer pepoptep.

There are three truly horrible letters. The letter Γ/γ is worse than it looks and different books give contradictory advice as to when it should be spoken as a sort of g and when it's closer to y. Γιώργος (George) is YOUR-goss and γυναίκα (woman) yi-NE-ka, at least to my ears. Then we have γλώσσα (tongue), GLO-sa, and γαλλικά (the French language) as ga-li-KA. Two common pieces of advice are *y before e and g before a* or *y before breakfast and g afterwards*. You can probably guess which one is mine.

The letter Ψ/ψ is the ps sound in *psst!* while Ξ/ξ is ks as in *ksst!* or box.

That's all the letters. Tip: If the word begins with w, you are not speaking Greek.

As part of my campaign to make the Greek language more accessible by reducing all words to three letters, a suggestion which one paper very rudely described as 'bul shi', I have also urged that each stress mark be replaced by a miniature of Picasso's *Guernica*. Until then, the stress is always on a vowel and you should try to get it right: Σπίτι (house) is SPI-tea and not spi-TEA. Getting it wrong would be like someone saying to us mar-KET rather than the correct MAR-ket, the sad difference being that in English mispronouncing a word can sound classy and educated whilst in Greek it comes across as foreign and thick which, indeed, most of us are.

And to remember all the letters in the first place? In English, 'A brown fox jumps quickly over the gold zebra' contains all 26 letters of the alphabet. In Greek, the shortest sentence is Ήρθε ο κύριος Βαγζλωμνξδπτφχψ (Mr Vagzlomnksthptfchps has come).

It's not too late to give up.

LESSON 3

When your toilet overflows:
Meeting neighbours for the first time

When the electricity wasn't working, Mr X, the handyman for my block of flats, came along with a few fuses.

When water from the shower was leaking through to my neighbour's bathroom, Mr X turned up to slap on some cement.

When an overflowing toilet was spewing raw sewage along my hallway, under the front door and into the building's main entrance, Mr X went to work with his amazing plunger.

And when, in the future, I report an outbreak of the limb-eating Ebola Disease, no doubt the amazing Dr X will be there with his anti-Ebola first aid kit. Truly, wherever you go in this world, you will never meet more resourceful (let us not say mis-guided) people than the Greeks.

In real emergencies, neighbours *(γείτονες)* are your lifeline. If the worst comes to the worst, you will definitely need to know *χρειάζομαι ένα ασθενοφόρο γρήγορα* (I need an ambulance quickly).

Be warned, it's a very difficult phrase to learn. My friend Andrew, a translator by profession, has two inexplicable prob-lems. One, he suffers from a manic compulsion to put the word 'elephant' into any text he sees, which explains why Queen Elizabeth didn't respond to my letter about her mother. Second, he always manages to confuse the Greek for ambu-lance with the word for daisy and no one can fathom out why.

The emergency operator even has a tape of Andrew ringing up and pleading pitifully:

Σας παρακαλώ, χρειάζομαι μία μαργαρίτα γρήγορα
Please, I need a daisy quickly

The result is that no one takes him seriously any more with the exception of Interflora.

For many foreigners, their first contact with neighbours will be that gentle battering on the door and a demand to pay the monthly common maintenance fees *(τα κοινόχρηστα)* for the apartment complex in which nearly all Athenians live. Or you might run into kids playing in the street. Children are a real blessing for learning Greek. Adults just think I'm unbelievably stupid whereas kids are far more tolerant of mistakes.

Try varying your greeting each day. Instead of *τι κάνετε;* (how are you?), choose the more informal *πώς πάει;* (how's it going?). I rarely get the chance since neighbours always open the conversation with *πώς λειτουργεί η τουαλέτα σας;* (how's your toilet?).

My toilet overflowed because I put paper down the bowl and blocked it up. Big mistake. Due to a poor sewage system, you're meant to place the 'used' paper in a bin next to the toilet. If this container is not within reach, you either make a paper airplane and try and glide it in - taking care in tavernas where the toilet has a big gap at the bottom of the door and is by the main dining area - or scrunch up the package and drop in a match-winning three-pointer. It's no coincidence that Greece is one of the best basketball-playing countries in the world and Luxembourg is not. All said and done, many foreigners decide to 'go' directly into the bin. Incidentally, if you discover, post-performance, that there's no toilet paper, have a delve through this bin. It's amazing what you'll find.

When chatting with neighbours, expect to be asked if you like Greece (yes you do). In this Christian nation, the next question will naturally concern your star sign.

As for dealing with the inevitable enquiry, *από πού είστε;* (where are you from?), read this little guide before answering:

(London)	*Είμαι από το Λονδίνο*	I'm from London
(New York)	*Είμαι από τη Νέα Υόρκη*	I'm from New York
(Ankara)	*Δε θυμάμαι*	I don't remember
(Skopje)*	*Είμαι από το Make... Λονδίνο*	I'm from Mace...London
(Glasgow)	*Είμαι από την Άγκυρα*	I'm from Ankara

In time, neighbours can become good friends. Years back, after a wonderful group meal, someone suggested a moonlight visit to the nearby Herodion amphitheatre, which is underneath the magical Acropolis and best known for being the place where Greek-American superstar Yanni recorded his famous concert.

In any other nation, 10 drunks at 3am asking the security guards if they could have a look at a beautiful, ancient, priceless monument wouldn't stand a chance. But allowed in we were and it was fantastic, one of my most pleasant memories of Greece. When the damage estimates have been finalised, my lawyer will be happy to say more on this subject. I would, however, like to apologise to Yanni's fans for having to stand throughout the evening.

* See Lesson 8 for explanation of this classy joke

NEVER PUT PAPER DOWN YOUR OWN TOILET

δε μιλάω τουρκικά . . . . .I don't speak Turkish
από πού είστε; . . . . .where are you from?
δεν είμαι από την Άγκυρα . . . . .I'm not from Ankara
πώς πάει; . . . . .how's it going?
ζήτω οι Κούρδοι! . . . . .long live the Kurds!
οι γείτονες . . . . .neighbours
δε θυμάμαι . . . . .I don't remember
χρειάζομαι ένα ασθενοφόρο . . . . .I need an ambulance
δεν έχω πάει ποτέ στην Τουρκία . . . . . . .I've never been to Turkey
πες μου! . . . . .tell me!

LESSON 4

Getting on the bus

Drive to work in Athens? Walk to work in Athens? Swim to work in Athens? Catch a train to work in Athens? Run to work in Athens? Motorbike to work in Athens? Hop on a trolley to work in Athens? Fly to work in Athens? Sail to work in Athens? This lesson is for all readers who work in Thessaloniki.

Actually it's for anyone who goes by bus *(με το λεωφορείο)* to work in Athens. One other group of people might find it helpful if the unconfirmed story, several years ago, about the tourist taken from the airport to the centre of Athens is true. At the end of the 30-minute taxi ride, the meter showed 400 (drachmas) which the victim was forced to pay - in dollars. You will be squashed to death on the bus, involved in several multiple pile-ups on the bus, stripped naked and savagely abused on the bus but, the great thing is, you will never be ripped off on the bus.

What you need to know above anything else is whether it's the *right* bus. There are some important clues.

First, it is the *wrong* bus if it pulls up alongside you when you are not standing at a bus stop *(στάση λεωφορείου* or just *στάση)*. The stops are easy to find as there's normally one every ten metres; a sponsored walk is not one of the best ways to raise money in Greece, though far better than a sponsored fast. Biblical scholars agree that Jesus was only able to feed the 5,000 because no Greeks were present.

Second, check you're on the correct side of the road because the same bus can go in two different directions and, in Athens, a third will often be attempted. Ask anyone nearby in basic Greek, *εδώ για X;* (here for X?). Substituting the place name for X is highly recommended.

Third, and a big help in making the right choice, both your bus and the stop sign are normally blue. Trolleys and their signs are yellow. That said, I have seen a blue trolley but I have never seen a yellow bus, notwithstanding a yellow trolley which I thought was a blue bus in disguise but it wasn't. Along with the Reverend Martin Luther King, Jr *(see Lesson 23)*, I have a dream of one day (altogether now, *one day!)* seeing little blue buses *(little blue buses!)* and little yellow trolleys *(little yellow trolleys!)* and little white vans *(little white vans!)* and little black cars *(little black cars!)* happily travelling along together but I doubt if the roads in Athens are wide enough. If you're colour blind, ask someone:

Με συγχωρείτε, τι χρώμα είναι αυτό το λεωφορείο;
Excuse me, what colour is this bus?

Don't be too despondent if the answer is not colour-related.

Fourth, always ask yourself: Is it a bus? Buses in Greece are like coaches, long but not high. If you have time and a tape measure *(μετροταινία* - literally 'underground film'), the blue bus is about two-and-a-half metres high and twelve metres long. For a second opinion, ask the same person you questioned about the colour (she or he will be used to you by now):

Πόσο μακρύ είναι το λεωφορείο;
How long is the bus?

If it all sounds very complicated, bear in mind that many people prefer to get on board at the terminal as they find this much easier than jumping on a moving bus. Also, you might well catch the driver in his seat, raring to go (home). This is a good time to ask questions like *πότε φεύγει;* (when does it [the bus] leave?) and *είναι ανάγκη να πίνετε τώρα;* (do you need to be drinking that now?).

Once the journey gets underway and intuition insists you've got on the wrong bus, quickly ask passengers *πού πάμε;* (where are we going?). When everyone's laughter has subsided, get ready for *πρέπει να πάρετε...* (you should take...) followed by the number of the bus *...το διακόσια πενήντα έξι* (...the 256). The number is normally said in full rather than specifying each digit (eg *δύο-πέντε-έξι*, 2-5-6). In keeping with the helpful nature of the Greek language, this means you have to learn from 1 to 999 rather than just up to nine. I wish they'd colour-code the buses. Kifissia? Take the Pine Meadow shade of Autumn Green. Easy.

Greece is the land of second chances so if you're not at a stop and suddenly see the bus approaching, do try your luck, particularly if the pavement gives you right of way. I remember being late for a really important interview and frantically waving at the driver whilst pulling out my 'Macedonia is Greek' banner. The kind man braked, sending thousands of passengers flying, and opened the front doors. Without getting on, I casually said *Τι ωραία μέρα σήμερα!* (What a lovely day today!) and got in the taxi behind.

IS THE BUS BLUE?

περνάει το λεωφορείο από 'δώ;	does the bus go past here?
κάνει εδώ στάση το λεωφορείο;	does the bus stop here?
η αφετηρία	terminal
το τρόλεϊ	trolley
από πού;	from where?
πού πάτε;	where are you going?
η μετροταινία	tape measure
ο οδηγός	driver
πόση ώρα είναι η διαδρομή;	how long is the journey?
τι χρώμα είναι αυτό το λεωφορείο;	what colour is this bus?

LESSON 5

Getting off the bus

In the previous lesson, we looked at the difficulties *(δυσκολίες)* in getting on a bus. In this lesson, we look at the difficulties *(δυσκολίες* in case you've already forgotten) in getting *off* a bus.

But, first, what happens on the bus itself? If you need a ticket, politely ask another passenger: *Μήπως έχετε κανένα εισιτήριο;* ('Do you happen to have a ticket?'). Or pretend to be a widely hated inspector and confidently shout out *τα εισιτήριά σας, παρακαλώ!* (your tickets please!).

Let's get one thing clear - drivers don't issue tickets. A few object to the presence of a steering wheel. There used to be an honesty box where people put in their fare. No, it wasn't nicked. But it was often ignored - the concept of voluntary donations not having caught on here - so now you have to get tickets, 120 drachmas each, from the normal yellow kiosks or special transport huts dotted around the city. Complicating things, some kiosks don't have such tickets while many huts display a notice, *Όχι εισιτήρια/No tickets.* The folks inside get real angry when asked so if each reader could do it just twice a day for me I'd be very grateful. A bus card, with unlimited travel, can save money, depending on the number of general strikes that particular month.

You validate your ticket by putting it in the orange machines which are deliberately positioned as far away as possible, the one on the roof being relocated only after hospitals warned their emergency wards were getting dangerously full. If the bus is 'crowded', officially defined as three people sitting in the driver's seat at the same time, murmur a simple *παρακαλώ* (please) and hand your ticket to the passenger next to you. He will give it to the bozo alongside him and so on until the ticket reaches the machine or window, whichever is the nearest. Or you can say *παρακαλώ, μου το χτυπάτε;* (will you punch it for me, please?), keeping your head at a safe distance. In the rare event you get your ticket back, *ευχαριστώ* (thank you) is nice.

Without a ticket you run the risk of being caught by a real inspector. This sub-species of mankind (I refuse to take sides on the issue) is common during the morning hours. If caught, you can do what any self-respecting Athenian does and argue that 'Just because I haven't got a ticket doesn't mean I haven't got a ticket. It simply means...' and at this point shout very loudly. A lot of politicians have started their careers this way.

Or you can go for a) *έχασα το εισιτήριό μου* (I lost my ticket) b) the honest *δεν έχω* (I don't have one), leading to an on-the-spot fine of around 4,800 drachmas and the possibility of being taken off to a police station if you can't pay, so I've heard c) *το μηχάνημα δε λειτουργεί* (the machine doesn't work) and run while he's trying it out d) *έχω διπλωματική ασυλία* (I have diplomatic immunity). Choose your country wisely, that's all I'll say.

Ticket trouble aside, one of the major problems on board is the lack of space. Occasionally you may feel truly frightened by the crush. If you're in a tight scrum at the back and it seems someone is deliberately getting too close, a simple *σιγά* may help, in this case meaning 'watch it'. Or just ask the driver to concentrate on the road.

Most signs on the bus are translated into English so you can readily understand the hammer is for breaking the window - *only in an emergency*, the publisher's lawyers have asked me to make clear. The hammer is rarely there but that's not really the point. There has been a subtle evolution in the messages displayed. The old-style buses, boasting a massive gear stick, have the prominent sign: *Μη μιλάτε στον οδηγό* (Don't talk to the driver). On the new buses, the order becomes much wider: *Μην ενοχλείτε τον οδηγό* (Don't bother/annoy the driver).

When it's time to get off, head for the middle or back doors - the driver's cigarettes often block the front exit - pressing a red 'stop' knob as you go. Should a passenger seem reluctant to move aside, murmur *θα κατεβείτε;* (will you get off?). If you're in an enormous hurry, where I come from this gentle English admonition often works:

GET OUT THE BLOODY WAY!

What should you do if the bus has reached your stop and the doors don't open? Shout *ανοίξτε!* (open!) to which you can add *την πόρτα* (the door) if you think there's any room for misunderstanding - the driver has a tin of pineapple chunks on his dashboard for example. You'll hear shouts of *πίσω* for the back doors and *μεσαία* for the middle.

And what if, in a land where a survey showed 85% of Greek motorists think a red traffic light means 'green is on its way', the driver doesn't pull in at the proper place? Breathe in and scream *στάση!* ('stop!'). It's as simple as that. Chances are he'll drive on.

ANYTHING I SAY WILL BE IGNORED

έχω διπλωματική ασυλία . . . . . .I have diplomatic immunity
τα εισιτήριά σας, παρακαλώ . . . .tickets please
ανοίξτε! .open!
θα κατεβείτε; . . . . .will you get off?
κατεβαίνετε; . . . . .are you getting off?
μήπως έχετε κανένα εισιτήριο; . .do you have a ticket?
δεν έχω .I don't have
θα κατέβω στην επόμενη στάση . .I'm getting off at the next stop
έχασα το εισιτήριό μου . . . . .I lost my ticket
ο ανανάς . . . . .pineapple

LESSON 6

Asking someone out

She's gorgeous *(πανέμορφη)*. He's cute *(γλυκούλης)*. That woman is perfect *(τέλεια)*. This man is fantastic *(απίθανος)*. And they're both Greek. Ah. And you don't speak any Greek. Er. And they don't speak much English. Oh.

Some psychologists claim we judge people within 30 seconds of meeting them for the first time - especially if they've just broken into our house - and that all subsequent contact makes no difference whatsoever. The only exception is wedlock, where proximity simply refines the hatred.

If the half-a-minute rule is true, we stuttering, tongue-tied, pronoun-fearing foreigners don't appear to have much of a chance. That said, this lesson tries to even out the odds a bit by covering situations where you might have the opportunity, however fleeting, to ask someone out - in Greek. The rest is up to you.

The one-off encounter demands quick action. You see Mr Right or Ms Wonderful knocked down in the street and you know you'll never step over them again. What to say? Easy, albeit a little direct, is *μου δίνεις το τηλέφωνό σου;* (can I have your telephone number?). If the answer is *δεν έχω τηλέφωνο* (I don't have a telephone), the truly lovestruck could try *μπορώ να σου αγοράσω ένα τηλέφωνο;* (can I buy you a telephone?).

It's more likely that the person you want to ask out is someone you regularly encounter at work, school, the supermarket, in court or at friends' parties. This at least gives you the chance to work out a few phrases in advance such as *πάω σινεμά την Παρασκευή. Ενδιαφέρεσαι;* (I'm going to the cinema on Friday. Are you interested?). For the English, a pathetically shy favourite is:

Θα 'θελες να βγούμε για καφέ μια μέρα;
Would you like (to go for) a coffee one day?

For readers still at school, a nice phrase, so I'm told, is *θες να τα φτιάξουμε;* (meaning 'will you be my boyfriend/girlfriend?'). If you're into romantic slush, memorise *είσαι όμορφη* (you're beautiful - when talking to a girl), *έχεις ωραίο χαμόγελο* (you have a lovely smile), *έχεις ωραίο αυτοκίνητο* (you have a lovely car) and *είσαι ο άντρας/η γυναίκα των ονείρων μου* (you're the man/woman of my dreams).

Okay, you've said all this but apparently not got anywhere. Don't despair. My famous 'Girlie for Churchie' four-stage approach nearly always elicits a response:

Τι κάνεις απόψε;	What are you doing tonight?
Τι κάνεις αύριο;	What are you doing tomorrow?
Τι κάνεις το Σαββατοκύριακο;	What are you doing at the weekend?
Τι κάνεις το 2006;	Any plans for 2006?

Still nothing? Go for it tiger!

Σε θέλω	I want you
Σε λατρεύω	I adore you
Σε χρειάζομαι	I need you
Σ' αγαπώ	I love you

Say *σας αγαπώ* if it's the president you've fallen for.

In a conservative setting, perhaps a small village up north, you may want to get the father's permission to ask his daughter out or, indeed, the daughter's permission to ask her father out. If the old man takes you into the barn and asks *πιστεύεις στις προγαμιαίες σχέσεις;* (do you believe in sex before marriage?), two answers to definitely avoid are *πιστεύω στο σεξ πριν από οτιδήποτε* (I believe in sex before anything) and *ευχαριστώ πολύ, αλλά για την κόρη σας ενδιαφέρομαι* (thank you very much but it's your daughter I'm interested in).

And how do you know if the person wants to go out with you? *Ναι* is yes, *όχι* is no and *ποτέ* is never (pronounced po-TEH, the po as in pot and the -TEH as in tent). Assuming you feel your ears tingling to the first response, your next question will be *πότε;* (when? - PO-teh) and *πού;* (where?), followed by signing of contracts with witnesses. *Εδώ* (here) is always a useful meeting place or, for non-vegetarians, *McDonald's στο Σύνταγμα* (McDonald's in Syntagma). As a general rule, the better the date goes, the less Greek you need to know.

If you really can't work up the courage to ask someone out face to face *(πρόσωπο με πρόσωπο)*, try writing him/her a letter in your native tongue. If they're keen enough, they'll always get it translated. But don't, whatever you do, enclose *ένα φάκελο με διεύθυνση και γραμματόσημο* (a stamped addressed envelope). It gives the wrong impression - in any language.

WORDS TO WHISPER BY CANDLELIGHT

σ' αγαπώ . . . . .I love you
σας αγαπώ . . . . .I love you (heads of state)
είσαι όμορφη . . . . .you're beautiful (to a girl)
έχεις ωραίο χαμόγελο . . . . .you have a lovely smile
έχεις ωραίο αυτοκίνητο . . . . .you have a lovely car
θα πληρώσεις; . . . . .will you pay?
μου αρέσεις . . . . .I like you
θα με παντρευτείς; . . . . .will you marry me?
θέλω διαζύγιο . . . . .I want a divorce
μπορώ να σου αγοράσω
    ένα τηλέφωνο; . . . . .can I buy you a telephone?

32

LESSON 7
Answering the phone

What's the best way to answer the phone in Greece? Pick up the receiver *(ακουστικό)* of course.

You've many choices after this vital first step, from the polite *παρακαλώ;* (close to 'can I help you?') or *ναι;* (yes?) to the more direct *λέγετε!* (speak!) and *εμπρός!* ('get on with it!' without the rudeness). Also heard is 'hello' in English. Or don't say anything! (I am indebted to my friends at the Athens Airport Tannoy Announcement & Public Information Division for this suggestion.)

At work, callers' first questions are typically *μπορώ να μιλήσω με τον κύριο X;* (can I speak with Mr X?). If you don't fully understand, and that's being generous, ask *ποιον θέλετε;* (who do you want?). And if he's not there? Choose between *μόλις έφυγε* (he's just left) and *μόλις βγήκε* (he's just gone/stepped out), the last one implying that the person will be back, ie he hasn't left for the day. *Μόλις πέθανε* (he's just died) suggests he may be gone for some time. If it's a salesman on the line, your atrocious mix of Greek and English can be very effective: *Θα πάρω two hundred and seventy πέντε* (I'll take 275) ends many a call or ensures your office will have more encyclopaedias than most.

If the person the caller asks for is, in fact, yourself, males should reply *ο ίδιος* (literally 'the same' - ie that's me) and females *η ίδια* ('that's me' as well). Do not phone yourself.

Make sure callers identify their nationality if there's any doubt. More than once I've struggled along in pidgin Greek, discussing the tautological development of Matisse's exploratory brushwork, before realising that we were both native English-speakers and immediately switching to Liverpool stuffing Spurs at the weekend.

To know who's calling, ask *το όνομά σας παρακαλώ;* (your name please?) or *ποιος/ποια τον/την ζητάει;* (who's asking for him/her?). Note *ποιος* if male caller, *ποια* if female, *τον* for him, *την* for her. It sounds difficult but the trick is to celebrate every little achievement as you go along. Follow the example of the Greek post office which issued a new set of stamps after the national soccer team won a corner at the 1994 World Cup. Remember: Michelangelo got nowhere trying to paint the ceiling of the Sistine Chapel until a friend suggested he use a ladder.

If you want to say 'please hold the line', 'wait a minute' or even 'I'll just get him', there's the all-embracing *μισό λεπτό* (half-a-minute) or, in a big building, *μιση μέρα* (half-a-day). For variation, *μια στιγμή* (one moment) is fine.

We now move on to a national institution, the wrong number, which in Greece, an Athenian told me, is often an excuse for a chat. Be careful. US serial killer and Cannibal Hall of Famer, Jeffrey Dahmer, sounded like a very nice young man over the phone.

To confirm he's dialled the wrong number - rather than as happens so very often in Greece the *right* number at the *wrong* time - the caller will say *Έχω πάρει το 3333555* (I dialled 3333555). You reply: *Όχι, αυτό το νούμερο είναι 9849340* (No, this number is 9849340).

As for how you give out the numbers, my friend Mary advises 'whatever sounds nicest but it has to rhyme somewhere'. I thought Mary was joking - she's from Chicago - but I'm told this is actually standard practice. Take my editor's home telephone number, 3666989 (pop on 30-1 for international calls). Mary recommends *τρία* (3), *εξήντα έξι* (66), *εξήντα εννιά* (69), *ογδόντα εννιά* (89) with the two nines rhyming. But her husband Tom prefers (they don't go out much) *τριάντα έξι* (36), *εξήντα έξι* (66), *εννιά-οκτώ-εννιά* (9-8-9). And if your phone number refuses to rhyme? Move.

34

Wherever you live, helpful phrases to learn exclude: *Το νούμερο που θέλετε είναι...* (The number you want is...); *λάθος νούμερο* (wrong number) or *έχετε κάνει λάθος* (you've made a mistake), both of which can earn the age-old reply *τότε γιατί το σηκώσατε;* (so why did you answer?, literally 'pick it up'); *δεν ξέρω που είναι* (I don't know where he is); *μπορείτε να ξαναπάρετε σε σαράντα εφτά λεπτά;* (can you call back in 47 minutes?); the very dangerous *θέλετε να αφήσετε κάποιο μήνυμα;* (do you want to leave a message?); and *είναι επείγον;* (is it urgent?). It always is.

Greeks love to talk (witness the recent mobile phone explosion) and can't understand anyone who doesn't share this passion. So few friends call me at home that those cheeky chappies at the state telecommunications company (OTE) occasionally ring to check if my phone is still working. Everyone refers to the telephonic giant as 'o-TEH' - the 'teh' bit as in teddybear and that's where the comparison ends.

Spend a day in Greece and you'll quickly notice that OTE tends to get the blame for anything that goes wrong. But the service is not so bad. As my brother in Spain said the other day, 'It's a very clear line' *(Η γραμμή είναι πολύ καθαρή)*. This was absolutely true even though I had actually dialled my uncle in Scotland.

WORDS I REALLY MUST TRY TO PICK UP

δεν σας ακούω	I can't hear you
μ' ακούτε;	can you hear me?
ξαναπάρτε!	ring again!
μιλήστε δυνατότερα/πιο δυνατά!	speak louder!
μιλήστε πιο σιγά/αργά	speak slower!
θα σας συνδέσω	I'll put you through
μιλάτε αγγλικά;	do you speak English?
η φρουτοσαλάτα	fruit salad
μιλάει αυτή τη στιγμή	he's talking at the moment
αντίο	goodbye

LESSON 8

Oh dear, politics

The old joke - two Greeks on a desert island form three political parties - has some truth to it. Greece can be a hard country to govern, a place where everything changes so quickly. 'Premier Costas Simitis' is one of the most daring phrases in this book. It was only a few years ago that newspapers used to have *Today's Cabinet* on their front page.

Simitis, in power since January 1996, is by all accounts a very curious prime minister *(πρωθυπουργός)*. In the past, if the press accused a leader of nepotism his cousin would look into the charges. No more. Many Greeks are astounded by Simitis' obvious willingness to take decisions which put the nation's interests first rather than his own popularity or that of the ruling party (Pasok/ΠαΣοΚ). Such abuse of office has never been seen before. Some say it might even be unconstitutional.

Pasok *(Πανελλήνιο Σοσιαλιστικό Κίνημα* - the Panhellenic Socialist Movement) was founded in 1974 by Andreas Papandreou who, as occupant of Maximos House *(Μέγαρο Μαξίμου)* for most of the 1980s, gave the country its pride back or bankrupted the economy, depending on your political viewpoint. Greece is doing better now. The government *(κυβέρνηση)* makes a lot of money from lotteries, if at least two cabinet ministers win each week.

Ο Πρόεδρος της Δημοκρατίας (President of the Republic), currently Costis Stephanopoulos, tops the political tree, albeit on a mainly ceremonial branch. Costas Karamanlis* is the leader of the opposition *(ο αρχηγός της αντιπολίτευσης).* His party, *Νέα Δημοκρατία* (New Democracy), was also founded in 1974 after the fall of the military dictatorship. Old Democracy didn't sound right.

Greek politics was once famously said to have three extremes: The extreme right, the extreme left and the extreme centre. Smaller parties, helped by minorities often being in the majority, never have trouble making themselves heard. Synaspismos *(Συνασπισμός της Αριστεράς*/Coalition of the Left) is forever asking for a meeting of party leaders. It doesn't matter what the subject is - from the outbreak of World War Three to a minister's dog lost in the national gardens - Synaspismos wants a meeting of party leaders. The Communist Party of Greece *(Κομμουνιστικό Κόμμα Ελλάδας)* is also known as KKE (you'll hear *kou-kou-eh*) or by saying its initials in full, *Κάππα Κάππα 'Εψιλον.* Thankfully Dikki doesn't do this. Dikki? Yes ΔΗΚΚΙ, the Democratic Social Movement *(Δημοκρατικό Κοινωνικό Κίνημα)*, not to be confused with the far more popular 'Never Heard of Them Movement'. The slightly nationalist party, *Πολιτική 'Ανοιξη* (Political Spring), is not represented in the current parliament.

Each political group in Greece has its own headquarters whose street names are used interchangeably with the party itself. Pasok meets in *Χαριλάου Τρικούπη* (Harilaou Trikoupi), ND in *Ρηγίλλης* (Rigillis), Dikki in *Χαλκοκονδύλη* (Halkokondili) and KKE in *Περισσός* (Perissos, the place). Synaspismos can be found in an unpronounceable square called *Κουμουνδούρου,* which explains the Coalition's lack of publicity these days. A meeting of party leaders has been requested. Political Spring followers gather in the nearest park.

Foreign affairs can dominate politics in Athens. The government often - and rightly - condemns long-time antagonist Turkey for human rights abuses such as jailing journalists and murdering Kurds. *(Important note to publisher: For our Turkish*

*Prime minister since March 2004

edition, please replace the entire last sentence with 'Both Greece and Turkey play basketball very well.')

While individual Greeks and Turks normally get on fine, it's a little more difficult for their leaders to meet and talk. Everything would change if the long-running Cyprus issue *(το κυπριακό πρόβλημα)* was solved by the removal of Turkish troops from the north and enforced rights for all Cypriots. Not that it's just Cyprus. Turkey, which tends to be needlessly aggressive, has warned Greece that if it extends its Aegean territorial waters to 12 nautical miles from the current six, as Athens kindly informs Ankara it has every right to do under international law, it will be war. Now what do they mean by that? I have suggested extending it to eleven and three quarter miles just to see what would happen.

Athens has also clashed with Skopje, the capital of a state which calls itself plain and simple Macedonia - exactly the same name as Greece's historic northern region next door. In the past you would see *Η Μακεδονία είναι ελληνική* (Macedonia is Greek) signs everywhere but the issue has almost died out now under the moderate Simitis. Confusing outsiders, Greece currently refers to its neighbour as the Former Yugoslav Republic of Macedonia (FYROM) and this is the name I always use but only because I'm paid by the word.

DON'T EVER ASK ANYONE ABOUT POLITICS

ο πρωθυπουργός . . . . .prime minister
οι βουλευτικές εκλογές . . . . .general election(s)
ο πληθωρισμός .inflation
η κυβέρνηση συνασπισμού . . . . .coalition government
το υπουργείο εξωτερικών . . . . .foreign ministry
η ανεργία . . . . .unemployment
η Ευρωπαϊκή Ένωση (ΕΕ) . . . . .European Union
η Βουλή . . . . .Parliament
ο βουλευτής . . . . .MP
ο Οργανισμός Ηνωμένων Εθνών (ΟΗΕ) . . .United Nations

LESSON 9

Telling the time (and other miracles)

You will never find out the correct time in Greece. Settle for something less ambitious like playing golf on Mars with Elvis.

In a survey of this column's readership, sponsored by the First Bank of Buenos Aires, people were asked how often they bought 6.41 percent, 15-year Argentine government bonds and why they wanted to learn Greek. The top three answers to the second question were: 'To fully appreciate the richness of this beautiful language' (2%), 'To join in my partner's family arguments' (88%) and 'To find out the time' (6%).

It's hard. Public clocks offer a bewildering choice. Almost nothing starts at the advertised time. Island buses leave when they leave. Meetings begin when people arrive. For the average Greek, seconds, minutes and hours fade in importance alongside coffee, cigarettes and chocolate croissants. Worried Westerners can only forget the clock when on holiday. Happy Hellenes can only remember the clock when cooking a chicken. As sociologists might say, there are major cultural differences at work here. Many foreigners automatically look at their watches when explicit sex scenes come on the TV not long after sunset.

If you arrive dead on time for a meeting, or even early, both of which are totally unacceptable, a Greek friend might unhappily murmur *Εγγλέζος/Άγγλος είσαι* (You're English). Stavropoulos the Great (see next lesson) gives *Είμαι Εγγλέζος στα ραντεβού μου*

('I'm an Englishman for my appointments') as '[to] be always very punctual'. If you arrange to meet a friend and he tells you *Είμαι Έλληνας [a Greek] στα ραντεβού μου*, take a book.

Still timeless? Talk to the Speaking Clock on 141. Like anywhere else, the recording is dull and lifeless:

Στον επόμενο τόνο, η ώρα θα είναι - ΠΕΤΡΟ, ΚΛΕΙΣΕ ΤΗ ΜΟΥΣΙΚΗ! - ένδεκα και πέντε και δέκα δευτερόλεπτα

On the next stroke, the time will be - PETER, TURN THE MUSIC OFF! - 11.05 and ten seconds

Occasionally it's you who will be asked *τι ώρα είναι;* (what's the time) or, more politely, *τι ώρα έχετε;* ('what time do you have?') and *έχετε ώρα;* (do you have the time?).

Be on your guard in Athens as loathsome sharks usually ask the time, in Greek or English, to make contact with their intended victims. Almost immediately comes the next question, 'Where you from?', followed by an invitation to meet dubious women and drink ludicrously expensive alcohol. The threat is real - 90% of the cover price of the book currently in your hands (anywhere else I don't want to know) is to pay for my small glass of orange juice.

Listen to the radio at the top of the hour, or the annoying introduction to virtually any TV report, and you're bound to hear *η ώρα είναι...* (the time is...). Face to face with a stranger in the street, it's more usual to say *είναι* (it is) followed by the time or your grandmother's favourite jam recipe, depending on how the day's gone. At 3.15 you can either play for time until the slightly easier *είναι τρεις και είκοσι* (it's 3.20) or memorise *τέταρτο*, meaning a quarter. So 3.15 is *τρεις και τέταρτο* while 2.45 is *τρεις παρά τέταρτο*.

The word *παρά*, 'minus' in this case, is used for anything after the half hour. *Πέντε παρά είκοσι* ('five minus 20', ie 20 to 5 and not minus 15) can alternatively be said as *τέσσερις και σαράντα* ('four and forty') or, as the joke goes, *οκτώ και πεντακόσια είκοσι* ('eight and 520', ie 4.40) not that anyone will understand you, which seems to be a recurring theme of our lives in Greece.

40

You need *μισή* for half past. *Είναι οκτώ και μισή* is half past eight or there's the simpler *οκτώμιση*.

As for pm and am in Greece, contrary to common belief these do not stand for *pre-meal* and *after-meal* (or *another meal*). Confusingly, am is *π.μ.* (*προ μεσημβρίας* - katharevousa Greek for pre-noon) while pm is *μ.μ.* (*μετά μεσημβρίαν* - after noon).

Time is not everything. All were gathered at the correct hour for the visit of an International Olympic Committee big shot when Athens was trying to get the 1996 Games. Important men and women, so the story goes, chatted at the bottom of the 21 steps leading up to the grand Old Parliament, inside which was an exhibition showing the capital's suitability to host the Olympics. Cameras were rolling and foreign media watching as the dignitaries began to walk up the steps. Arriving at the top, they found the large wooden doors were...locked.

The unconfirmed tale, which is possibly true, ended with a frantic search for the building's caretaker. To Greece's great surprise, key-wise Atlanta got the Games. Fortunately, lessons were learnt and Athens' winning 2004 bid impressed everyone with its obvious professionalism and lack of visits to the Old Parliament.

TIME TO LEARN SOME WORDS

τι ώρα είναι;	what's the time?
δε σας λέω	I'm not telling you
είναι μιάμιση	it's 1.30
τα μεσάνυχτα	midnight
το μεσημέρι	noon
σε μισή ώρα	in half-an-hour
πέντε παρά πέντε	4.55 ('5 minus 5')
οκτώ παρά είκοσι επτά	7.33 ('8 minus 27')
δέκα παρά τέταρτο	quarter to 10
δέκα και τέταρτο	quarter past 10

LESSON 10

Sweet, succulent
and just asking for it

Έχει μεγάλο στήθος

Or, as the highly respected *Oxford Greek-English Learner's Dictionary* puts it, 'She has a big bust/bosom, she's big-busted, she's big round the bust' (Page 819). Yes okay, we get the point.

D.N. Stavropoulos' dictionary instantly became my new bible when I arrived in Greece though the language is far fruitier, particularly some of the examples which are surely an in-house joke. Witness the word *αδιάπλαστος/not formed/shaped, not [fully] developed* on Page 12 for which what better example than:

Το στήθος της ήταν ακόμα αδιάπλαστο
Her breasts were not fully developed yet

No need for any reference to a child's personality or a plan taking shape. If it really is a long-running wheeze, my hat comes off to those Oxonian rascals. I envy them. Secret messages used to go to and fro on the old *Athens News* pages without anyone ever noticing until an extra-sharp reader complained about a headline: *PLO kill Israeli soldier as Derek, Fancy a coffee later? Cheers, Brian.* And the subtitle really gave it away. What memories! We'd be using crosswords from British tabloids and a dear old lady from Kentucky, US of A, would ring up to say she really had no idea what the fifth largest town in Derbyshire was. Nor could she guess Prince Charles' favourite toffees. And as for that dreadful day when we accidentally printed the wrong set of answers so that 17 across, *Oscar-winning comedy*, appeared to be *Schindler's List*...

I digress but then so does Stavropoulos. I found myself reading the dictionary day and night, from *λάγνα κουνήματα/ lascivious swaying of hips* (illustrating the word 'lascivious') on Page 490 to *την ξέντυσαν και την πέταξαν στο νερό* (they stripped her naked and threw her into the water) 116 pages later.

Only for my really loyal readers did I dare look up:

Πέος - Το πέος του ήταν ακόμα αδιάπλαστο
Penis - His penis was not fully developed yet

To be fair, there aren't many languages boasting a verb like *ξεπορτίζω* (Page 607), which Stavropoulos initially defines as 'seduce somebody away from home'. My puzzled Greek friends insist his second definition, 'slip out, go away from home', with negative overtones, is the appropriate one.

Through it all, we have a poet struggling to escape a life in dictionaries, offering stirring language such as *το πεζοδρόμιο ήταν γεμάτο ροχάλες* (the pavement was spattered with spittle) which graces Page 774. That's gob to you and me. And never let it be said he doesn't explain a word: *Κροτώ/snap, crack, clack, tap, thud, thump, boom, rumble, thunder, bang, plop, pop, clank, clatter, patter, rattle, clang, jangle, jingle, click* (Page 482). Gosh, wouldn't want to play this guy at Scrabble.

Back to the ruder stuff with yet another spot-on example, this time for the expression *μου αρέσει* (I like). What do you think: Swimming or reading or living in London? Well, yes, all those are mentioned on Page 121, with the reading being in bed, but let's not omit *του αρέσουν πολύ τα μικρά* (he has a penchant for young girls).

Then a mate advised checking out Page 376 where Stavropoulos shows his sensitive side:

Για να μην τον θίξω δε μίλησα για τη βρόμα την αδερφή του
To spare his feelings I didn't talk about his bitch of a sister

St Augustine's just war concept of suffering being in proportion to the conflict could be adapted to regulate the use of examples in a dictionary - the ruder they get, the less relation they need have to the word being illustrated. Killjoys would just censor them altogether. In Iran, I'm told, Stavropoulos' 995-page blockbuster is sold in booklet form.

Another jewel illustrates καμαρώνω (to take pride in). Forget the kids doing well at school or your garden voted best in the village, there is only one possible choice: Καμάρωνε που είχε πάρει τη γυναίκα του φίλου του (He preened/plumed/piqued/ prided himself on having seduced his friend's wife, Page 410).

Don't get me wrong. There are some words he's fully entitled to wallow in. Γδύνω (to undress) on Page 182 reveals splendid use of 'and': Την έγδυσαν και... (They stripped her of her clothes and...). Page 771 also impresses with μου ρίχτηκε/μου τα 'ριξε στα ίσια αμέσως μόλις βγήκε ο άντρας της από το δωμάτιο (she gave me the come-on as soon as her husband was out of the room). Illustrating 'room' if you must know.

'To make a pass at' actually and I confess I made up the πέος example but all the others are real. Ditto the 10 below where, as throughout this lesson, both the Greek and English come straight from the master (Eighth impression, 1996). This dictionary will become a cult classic, mark his words.

WORDS I MUSTN'T SHOW MY MOTHER

ο παίδαρος .... big healthy boy, beefy youngster
η γυναικάρα .... strapping/buxom woman
η μπανάνα .... banana
ο άνδρας μου .... my man, my husband, my hubby
η καμπυλότητα της γης .... the curvature of the earth
γυναίκα με καμπυλότητες ..... curvaceous woman
τσίτσιδος .... stark naked
το πιροσκί .... sausage roll
πολύ μπάνικο κομματάκι! ..... isn't she a snazzy bit of skirt!
πολιτική αντιπληθωριστική ... anti-inflationary policy

LESSON 11

Giving directions & the art of lying

We've all suffered. You're in the street *(στο δρόμο)* when a car pulls up and the driver asks for directions. Sometimes the passenger asks for directions and the driver for a chocolate chip cookie but this shouldn't affect your answer.

Often you fail to understand the question being asked or don't know the street they want. It's very depressing when you *do* understand the question, *do* know where the street is but *don't* know how to explain it in Greek. Even worse is when you fully understand the question, know exactly where the street is, can give directions in beautiful, colourful Greek but then find out the driver only speaks Polish. Deadlock. You are Poles apart.

For what they're worth, a few tips on giving directions. Say *είμαι ξένος* (I'm a foreigner) and the car's normally reversed away at 200kph before you've had time to add *και αγαπάω την Ελλάδα* (and I love Greece - see Lesson 14). Also acceptable are *δεν ξέρω* (I don't know), *δεν είμαι από 'δώ* (I'm not from here) or *είμαι ξένος εδώ* (I'm a stranger to these parts), and *δεν μπορώ να σας βοηθήσω* (I can't help you). You could get the loony bells ringing with *το διαβατήριό σας παρακαλώ* (your passport please!) but don't try this anywhere near the border. (Greece, incidentally, is still an incredibly safe place despite growing crime rates and 70% of Europe's murders arising out of land disputes in Crete.)

If you're feeling in a bad mood, there's always *ξέρω 'γώ;* (how should I know?), *φύγε!* (go away) or, in the last resort, *είμαι εδώ*

για το συνέδριο της Μοσάντ (I'm here for the Mossad convention).
If the driver replies *και 'γώ* (me too), walk on calmly but quickly.

Another tactic is to use a standard answer. The basic verb when giving directions is *στρίβω* (to turn) which becomes *θα στρίψεις/θα στρίψετε* (you will turn). Pointing in the direction to go and using the friendly 'you' form for maximum psychological effect, confidently assert:

Στο δεύτερο δρόμο θα στρίψεις αριστερά, μετά ευθεία, έπειτα θα πάρεις τον πέμπτο δρόμο δεξιά, κοντά στην ψαροταβέρνα
Take the second left, go straight on and then take the fifth right near the fish taverna

Whatever you do, don't forget the fish taverna. It adds a touch of authenticity to your directions which will go down well. By the time they're hopelessly lost, you will be long gone and they can do what they should have done in the first place - ask a Greek.

There is a subtle alternative to this strategy: *Στο δεύτερο δρόμο θα στρίψεις αριστερά και μετά ευθεία μέχρι να δεις μια ψαροταβέρνα* (Take the second left and go straight on until you see a fish taverna). At this point you suddenly stop talking. In all likelihood, the driver will then ask *κι από 'κεί είναι κοντά;* (and it's near there, is it?) to which you respond:

Όχι, αλλά έχει πολύ καλό ψάρι
No, but it's very good fish

The Basques, who eat a lot of fish, sometimes give directions by telling people to go uphill or downhill rather than left or right, so I've heard. This doesn't work in Holland. Stepping on the silliness, an American comedian once pulled over in his car and asked a member of the public if she knew the way to Adams Street. The woman politely said she had no idea and was then baffled to hear the driver reply: 'Well, if you go up this road and take the first right...' You could try this on your last day in Greece.

Time to help our fellow citizens - *a giant cockroach, the*

*worst thing about life in Greece by far, especially if it flies, has
just appeared in front of my eyes at home as I write. Do I be an
Englishman and try and reason with it, an American and sue it,
a Frenchman and add it to my salad or a Greek and belt the hell
out of it? (pause) I really can't make up my THWACK, THWACK,
THWACK, THWACK, THWACK, SMASH, THWACK, THWACK,
THWACK, THWACK, THWACK, THWACK, THWACK, it's gone -*
in their hour of need. Learn the names of these local landmarks:
Η ταβέρνα (taverna), *το εστιατόριο* (restaurant), *το οινοποιείο*
(wine factory), *το τετράγωνο* (block, *δύο τετράγωνα* = two blocks),
το αστυνομικό τμήμα (police station), *η εκκλησία* (church), *το
ταχυδρομείο* (post office), *το Μνημείο του Άγνωστου Στρατιώτη*
(Tomb of the Unknown Soldier), THWACK, *το βενζινάδικο* (petrol
station), *το φανάρι* (traffic light), *το στενό* (side-street), *η γωνία*
(corner), *ο κεντρικός δρόμος* (main road) and *η πλατεία* (square).

At the end of the day, there's only one failsafe way in coping
when people ask for directions. Learn this phrase and learn it well:

Θα έρθω μαζί σου/σας
I'll come with you

IF IN DOUBT, SAY STRAIGHT ON

η ψαροταβέρνα	.fish taverna
ξέρω 'γώ;	.how should I know?
θα σε/σας πάω εγώ	.I'll take you there myself
φύγε!	.go away!
lehen mendian joan eskuimetara	go right at the first mountain
στρίβω	.to turn
δεν είμαι από 'δώ	.I'm not from here
καθ' οδόν	.on the way to/in the direction of
το Μνημείο του	
Άγνωστου Στρατιώτη	.Tomb of the Unknown Soldier
το Μνημείο του	
Άγνωστου Φορολογουμένου	.Tomb of the Unknown Taxpayer

LESSON 12

100 verbs

A verb a day keeps the noun away. If you can get your verb right, there's always the chance you won't need to finish your

In a couple of decades we'll start looking at how to form the various tenses but for this lesson I promised you 100 verbs. And the first of these 33 is *ψεύδομαι* (to lie). Don't get angry. This column/book *ανήκει σε μένα* (belongs to me). If I want to cheat *(εξαπατώ)* I shall. It's as simple as that.

And don't send someone round to get your money back. I know all the tricks, like the debt collector who appeared close to expiry date and so always got paid within seconds of tottering onto the debtor's premises. With millions of forms to fill in if someone drops dead on your territory, only big businesses can survive.

On with the verbs, which are given in the first person, present tense. You've no idea what I'm talking about but since you've already bought the book I really don't care. Why do you think this is Lesson 12 rather than Lesson 1? If you're still with me, here are 10 verbs you have to know: *Κάνω* (do, make), *πάω/πηγαίνω* (go), *θέλω* (want), *έχω* (have), *είμαι* (to be), *παίρνω* (take), *ξέρω* (know), *λέω/λέγω* (say, tell), *υποβάλλω αγωγή διαζυγίου* (file for divorce) and the important *μπορώ* (can) as in this example:

μπορώ-μπορώ

This means either the speaker's got a stutter or he's referring to an extremely famous dance (the cancan, with many apologies).

Κάνω has scores of different uses including *κάνω το βλάκα* (play the fool) and *τα κάνω θάλασσα* (make a mess of something). It's also the most popular conversation opener (or stopper) as in *τι κάνεις;* or *τι κάνετε;* (how are you?).

Πάω is almost as common: *Πού πας;* (where are you going?), *πού πήγες;* (where did you go?) and *πάμε!* (let's go!); the latter means *action!* when shouted by film directors. I teach you so much. *Έχω* is heard everywhere and forms the base for the perfect and pluperfect tenses, whatever they are. I teach you so little.

You've 'learnt' 13 verbs so far. Take the next month off work and try to memorise the following: *Νομίζω* (think), *έρχομαι* (come, arrive - *ήρθε*, he came; *έλα!*, come!), *βγαίνω* (go/come out - *βγες έξω!*, get out!), *καταλαβαίνω* (understand), *βλέπω* (see, look - *τι είδες;* what did you see?; *θα δούμε*, we'll see), *φεύγω* (leave - *έφυγε*, he left; *θα φύγω στις έξι*, I'll leave at six), *καίω* (burn), *δουλεύω* (work), *πληρώνω* (pay), *μιλώ/μιλάω* (talk, speak) and, of course, *τρώω/τρώγω* (eat - *έφαγα*, I ate).

Πληρώνω is an important verb but insignificant compared to *ασφαλίζω* (insure). Ahead of the marriage of George Best, his future father-in-law, worried by the footballer's boozy past, asked Lloyd's of London to insure the reception drinks bill.

As for *καίω*, this unfortunately is the key verb in summer when fires, many started by arsonists, rage throughout Greece. The verb rekindles itself on Bonfire Night *(η 5η Νοεμβρίου)*, marking the time Rome-supporting Guy Fawkes *(Γκάι Φόκς)* very naughtily tried to blow up the English parliament in 1605. To this day, international schools in Athens let off fireworks and light bonfires for the traditional burning of the guy, Fawkes' effigy. The same night, a few thousand kilometres away in High Wycombe, where Churchill's gardener was born, we really get into the historical spirit of things and toss on a few Catholics as well. They don't mind. We treat them well the rest of the year and they know it's just a few over-enthusiastic locals letting off steam.

That's 25 down, 8 to go. One way to remember verbs is to group them together. All of the following begin with the same letter. Can you guess which letter that is and which verb has been made up: *Ακούω* (hear, listen), *ακολουθώ* (follow), *αγγίζω* (touch), *αμίγω* (sleep with your best friend in the Balearic Islands after a particularly good tuna salad on a foggy Friday evening) and *αποφασίζω* (decide). Take your time.

Μην αγγίζετε! normally means 'don't touch!' (you thought *αγγίζω* was the made-up one?) but the entrance doors of an embassy in central Athens beg to differ. They bear a classy metallic notice with the immortal translation, *Keep your hands off!*

Many verbs are linked to nouns and adjectives. Or are the nouns and adjectives linked to the verbs? I've no idea, you'd have to ask a teacher. But I can give you an example. We've seen *αποφασίζω* is 'to decide' (this was your second choice?). The adjective *αποφασισμένος* means 'decided'. I impress myself.

Unsurprisingly, Athens, the last bastion of serious lunacy in an increasingly sensible Europe, has some exclusive verbs which are heard only within its confines, such as *φωνάζω* (shout), *απειλώ* (threaten), *καταγγέλλω* (file a complaint) and *οδηγώ στο μονοπάτι* (drive on the path).

I STILL THINK IT'S ΑΓΓΙΖΩ

αλλάζω	to change
ελπίζω	to hope
τα έκανα θάλασσα	I messed (it) up
δε σου κάνει	it doesn't fit you
δε σου πάει	it doesn't suit you
πάμε;	shall we go/leave?
τα λέμε	we'll talk (see you again)
θα δούμε	we'll see
θα ήθελα άλλο ένα ουίσκι	I would like another whisky
αρχίζω	to begin

LESSON 13

Greek-Spanish for English speakers

If Spain *(Ισπανία)* had an equivalent column to *Learn Greek in 25 Years*, it might well be called *Learn Spanish in 25 Seconds*.

This isn't knocking the language. On the contrary *(αντίθετα/ todo lo contrario)*. Spanish is beautiful because it's simple and it's simple because it's beautiful. If you can handle Greek, you can easily learn Spanish. And if you can speak Spanish, you can swiftly master Portuguese.

Lucky for some, this thirteenth lesson *(μάθημα/leccion)* is for my many Spanish and Latin American readers who I know would appreciate a few phrases from the world's leading quadrilinguist (Greek, English, Spanish and Swearing). For those struggling enough with Greek, and who hadn't even considered learning Spanish, read on! You never know, you might be a natural.

It's quiz time again. To find out how much of an intuitive feel you have for the language, look at the following Spanish words and try to guess their meaning:

el piano - el eclipse solar - el astronauta - el grupo de turistas

How many did you get? Pat on the back for more than one but don't worry if you found them too hard. Now for the same words in Greek:

το πιάνο - η έκλειψη ηλίου - ο αστροναύτης - η ομάδα τουριστών

The sad thing is that all these Greek words would be easily

understandable if we only knew how to read the letters. All too often we know that we don't know the word but, frustratingly, sometimes we don't know that we *do know*, if you know what I mean, which you probably don't.

Spanish might be easier to learn than Greek but not for everyone. Spare a thought for dog-breeders who move to Spain. There's no quarantine *(καραντίνα/cuarentena)* but imagine not speaking the language and having to go to night school four times a week to learn impossible names like:

el chow-chow

Chemists can suffer too - *tabla periodica* could be anything - and let's not forget journalists desperately trying to find out the meaning of *microfono* and *eleccion*.

The good news is that Greek and Spanish share many similar words. Look at *βάρκα (barca*/boat), *ρολόι (reloj*/watch), *καπετάν (capitan*/captain), *μπάνιο (bano*/bath), *γάγγραινα (gangrena*/gangrene) and *Σκωτσέζος (escoces*/Scotsman). The two sun-kissed tongues also have that phrase loved by civil servants struggling valiantly to fit molehills of work into their 40-minute week - *αύριο (manana)*. Strictly speaking, the English translation is 'tomorrow' but 'Come back in 125,000 years' is closer to the real meaning.

And both vocabularies are very expressive. For toilet, Spanish offers the colourful *excusado* and *retrete*. This last word should not be confused with a retreat *(retiro)* like Camp David *(Καμπ Ντέηβιντ)*, the US president's mountain home, itself the subject of several complaints from ultraorthodox Jews.

There are other bonds. Both nations seem linguistically reluctant to define when the afternoon *(απόγευμα/tarde)* ends and the evening *(βράδυ/tarde)* begins. Spain switches at about 5pm while Greece is any time after 2.30 in the morning.

Most importantly of all, each language contains a letter specially designed to deter foreigners. Amnesty International is currently campaigning for the Greek 'γ' to be outlawed by the European Court of Human Rights while the Spanish are constantly criticised for rolling their 'r's in such a sadistic and superior manner. Most beginners practise with *cigarrillo* (*τσιγάρο*/cigarette), *perro* (*σκύλος*/dog) and *piedra* (*πέτρα*/stone). True, this last word isn't normally rolled but *piedrrrrrrrrrrr-rrrrrrrrrrrrrrrrrrrrrrrrrrrrrrrrrrrrrrrrrrrrrrrrrrrrrrrrrrrrrr-rrrrrrrrrrrrrrrrrrrrrrrrrrrrrrrrrrrrrrrrrrrrrrrrrrrrrrrrrrrrrr-rrrrrrrrrrrrrrrrrrrrrrrrrrrrrrrrrrrrrrrrrrrrrrrrrrrrrrrrrrrrrr-rrrrrrrrrrrrrrrrrrrrrrrrrrrrrrrrrrrrrrrrrrrrrrrrra* is interesting because if you do it well enough you end up with Mick Jagger, a Rolling Stone. *Lo siento mucho (λυπάμαι πολύ*/I'm very sorry). A cheap trick for taking up your time and my page. Unacceptable *(απαράδεκτος/inaceptable)*.

Still on apologies, please forgive the lack of accents on some Spanish words in this lesson, including that squidgy thing which goes over the 'n' in *bano* or *excusado*. It sounds dreadful but we really couldn't be bothered to look them up in the computer character map - *la mapa caractica* or something similar. That's the joy of Spanish. If you don't know the word *(λέξη/wordo)*, you just make it up.

WORDS I REALLY MUST TRY TO APRENDER

Μαδρίτη	Madrid	*Madrid*
Ελλάδα	Greece	*Grecia*
Αθήνα	Athens	*Atenas*
εντάξει	okay	*vale/de acuerdo*
η πέτρα	stone	*la piedra*
το πιάνο	piano	*el piano*
βεβαίως	of course	*por supuesto*
καλημέρα	good morning	*buenos dias*
δεν είναι δυνατόν	it's not possible	*no es posible*
το τσάου-τσάου	chow chow	*el chow-chow*

LESSON 14

'If the firemen find a cigarette lighter...'

Greece has always been an advanced society. Long before e-mail or even Morse code, this country had perfected the art of communication. Just as strong today, the ingenious system doesn't use super-powerful computers or ultrasophisticated satellites. It uses *people*.

Take the manuscript of this book. To get the Greek checked by my friend Rena, who lives on an island, I had to see her sister, Maria, who was planning to visit Rena later that week. But Maria told me she was going to be out the afternoon I was going to be in her area of Athens. So we arranged I would leave the book in a garage opposite her block of flats and that she would pick it up later. However, if Sokratis, the mechanic to whom I was to give the package, had been called away, Maria said that I could hand it to... you get the idea. And it works! Rena got a Ford manual to check over and a proud new car owner is currently trying to make sense of the first five chapters of this book. Actually, no kidding, Rena now tells me her sister couldn't come out so she took the manuscript and passed it on to a doctor going to the island who, in turn, gave it to three more people, including a taxi driver, before arrival at Rena's, all within half a day.

In such an interactive society, the need will arise at some point THWACK to write a letter, the subject of this lesson. Short and simple is often the best approach. After Makis had passed some extremely tough exams, Hamish sent him this lovely message: *Συγχαρητήρια και εις ανώτερα! Παρακαλώ, μην ξεχνάς ότι ακόμη μου χρωστάς 50 δραχμές* (Congratulations and here's to your further success! Please don't forget that you still owe me 50 drachmas).

Personally speaking, I've always wanted a friend to qualify as a sauna operator so I could express my *Θερμά συγχαρητήρια* (Warm congratulations). Unfortunately, up till now my only letter in Greek has been to a friend's parents, apologising for exuberant behaviour at a party the night before:

Λυπάμαι πολύ γι' αυτό που έγινε. Εύχομαι να βρείτε καινούργιο σπίτι. Υ.Γ. Αν οι πυροσβέστες βρήκαν έναν αναπτήρα...
I'm very sorry for what happened. Good luck in finding a new house. P.S. If the firemen find a cigarette lighter...

For a challenge, you could always try and get a letter published in a Greek paper or magazine. Correspondence from foreigners is still a novelty and our chances are good if we say nice things about the country. Above all, your letter needs to be real and heartfelt. So let's make something up:

Ο φίλος μου φώναζε όλη την ώρα: 'Οι Αλβανοί θα μας σκοτώσουν όλους.' Μια νύχτα, στ' αστεία, διέρρηξα το σπίτι του με ένα όπλο και φορώντας μια μάσκα. Προς μεγάλη μου λύπη, πέθανε από καρδιακή προσβολή. Τι να κάνω τώρα; Μπράιαν, Κορυδαλλός
Υ.Γ. Είμαι ξένος και αγαπώ την Ελλάδα
My friend was always shouting: 'The Albanians will kill us all.' One night, for a joke, I broke into his flat with a gun and wearing a mask. To my great regret, he died of a heart attack. What do I do now? Brian, Korydallos Prison
P.S. I'm a foreigner and I love Greece

Many letters are in response to something received, a fact reflected in a typical opening to correspondence: *Ευχαριστώ για το γράμμα σας της 21ης Φεβρουαρίου 1986 το οποίο μόλις έφθασε εδώ* (Thank you for your letter of 21 February 1986 which has just arrived). Regarding endings, 10 suggestions are given in the list of words below.

As for signing a letter, this can be a dilemma since real names are rare in Greece. Consider this: My exterior door bell, utility bills and bank cash card are united by the total absence of the name 'Church'. When I first moved in I couldn't be bothered to unscrew my slot on the list of names at the entrance. After years of practice, I now automatically respond to and order pizzas in the name of 'Slawinska'. It's hard to describe the feelings of guilt when I meet an old Pole peddling perfumes and all he wants to do is talk about the Warsaw Uprising. Electricity, phone and water bills are under three different names - it's simply not worth the hassle trying to change them.

Even my cash card, which works regardless, has never quite got the name right. Originally it was Bria*m* Church, briam being a Greek summer dish, then an imaginative leap took it to C.B. Philip, the new surname being my middle name, the first initial my surname and the middle initial my first name. The current card, plain C. Philip, is encouraging. Stay here long enough and I might even get my 'Brian' back. I could write the bank a letter of complaint but what name would I sign it with?

ELEPHANT

Περιμένω απάντησή σας	I await your reply
Με εκτίμηση	Regards
Περιμένω ακόμα απάντησή σας	I still await your reply
Με τιμή/Μετά τιμής	With respect
Έχω ένα πολυβόλο	I have a machine gun
Ειλικρινώς υμέτερος	Sincerely yours
Με αγάπη	With love
Με τις καλύτερες ευχές	Best wishes
Ο φίλος σου	Your friend
Ο μόνος φίλος σου	Your only friend

LESSON 15

O happy day!

Καλό μήνα!

You don't understand, do you? Happy month, thicko. It's what you say in Greece on the first day of the month. Let's pretend, eh?

Our sunny-natured Greek friends are always wishing us 'kalo' something or other. Every day you'll hear *καλημέρα* (good morning, good day). Around midday there's *καλό μεσημέρι* ('happy noon'). *Καλό βράδυ* tends to be in the late afternoon, as a way of saying goodbye; *καλησπέρα* is for the early evening when you meet people. Feel free to chuck a 'you' in the middle of all these happy greetings for familiarity and emphasis: *Καλή σου νύχτα* (Good night to you).

An important detour. In media circles, all this pleasantness can be misleading. One of the great joys of Greek TV is watching small fringe stations interview foreign visitors, often an American academic making his first trip to Athens. Set in a posh hotel on a balmy Sunday evening, politely introduced and cordially thanked for coming, the distinguished professor has no idea of the fate awaiting him. When the translator relays the interviewer's first question - 'Would our learned guest kindly explain to the station's [three] viewers how the water shortage might be the basis of future conflict in the Middle East?' - the victim relaxes even further and gives a scholarly view on the rationing of resources and the need for coordination of public policy imperatives.

Only when the next question has been matter-of-factly

translated - 'Are the Jews trying to take all the water?' - do you see his smile suddenly vanish and sweat appear on the forehead as the reality of the situation hits home with much worse still to come. All in all, a bad start to the week for the professor, terrified the tape will get back to his university, funded by we know who.

Too late, then, to wish him *καλή εβδομάδα* (have a good week) which is said to friends and colleagues at the start of a new week and to me when I turn up for work on Wednesday. For the weekend, it's *καλό Σαββατοκύριακο* (happy weekend). Rarer is *καλή Κυριακή* (happy Sunday) if there's not much of the weekend left which, if you work for a daily paper, is sadly the case. The best definition of life as a journalist came in a note left by my mate Dino at 1am: 'Good night. See you today.' As I have brilliantly observed, the basic problem with journalism is that readers have more time to read than writers have to write. Books too. And sex.

Enough of the complaints. If it's dark and cold outside, you won't want to hear *καλό καλοκαίρι* (happy summer) or *καλές διακοπές* (happy holidays). Year-round wishes are *καλή διασκέδαση* (have a good time), *καλή διαμονή* (have a good stay) and *καλό ταξίδι* (have a good trip). *Καλό δρόμο* ('good road') wishes someone a safe and enjoyable car journey. A general greeting of goodwill when seeing someone for the first time after the holidays is *καλό χειμώνα* (literally 'happy winter').

Nicest of all phrases for us soppy Westerners is *καλά Χριστούγεννα* (Happy Christmas). *Καλή χρονιά* (Happy New Year) is uttered, unsurprisingly, on January 1 and when first meeting people thereafter, within reason. *Χρόνια πολλά* (may you enjoy 'many years') is also used for the New Year and on an individual's 'name day'. Nearly everyone here has the name of a saint. When the Orthodox Church calendar celebrates that saint, it's only fair all his namesakes should join in and the day is usually considered more important than a birthday. Most Greeks bear the same name as one of their grandparents which is why you meet a lot of nice young men called Brenda.

Know anyone who's got engaged? It's *καλά στέφανα,* which are the rings of flowers you bung on the head during the wedding ceremony. Know anyone who's getting married? *Καλή τύχη* (good luck - see Lesson 20 for more appropriate language). Know anyone who's died? *Καλή κηδεία* (have a good funeral) will guarantee a comprehensive casket-sharing thumping from surviving relatives.

Food has its own good collection with *καλή όρεξη* (bon appetit) as you start and the old-fashioned *καλή χώνεψη* when you finish. It means 'good digestion' in case you were wondering.

Καλή επιτυχία ('good success') is for anyone about to take a driving test, sit exams or go for an interview. When a friend has bought a car, new furniture or even a house, *καλορίζικο* ('may it be good luck') is common.

Καλή αντάμωση is a very warm 'till we meet again' preferred by the older generation. *Στο καλό* (effectively 'all the best') and *να είσαι καλά* ('be well') are used every day.

It's worth trying to get to know a few members of the Good family since you'll hear and bump into them everywhere. In my local supermarket they have a big notice, *Καλή σχολική χρονιά* (Happy new school year), just next to *Εκτελούμε τους κλέφτες* (We execute shoplifters).

GOOD FINE WORDS I REALLY MUST TRY TO LEARN

καληνύχτα	good night
καλή ιδέα	good idea
καλή δύναμη!	have courage!
καλοζώ	to live well
καλή τύχη	good luck
καλή θέληση	goodwill
το καλαμπόκι	sweet corn ('good bocki')
καλό Πάσχα	happy Easter
καλή εβδομάδα	have a good week
καλό ταξίδι	have a good trip

LESSON 16

George Bernard So:
How the Greeks see the English

Day and night. Chalk and feta cheese. Crete and gun control. Athens and vegetarianism. The Greeks *(οι Έλληνες)* and the English *(οι Άγγλοι)*. Total opposites.

The difference can be dramatic. A Greek friend was stunned to discover that part of the sea *(θάλασσα)* in southern England was *closed*, with a notice to this effect put up on a large fence by the management of an adjacent shopping complex.

Take an Englishman and a Greek sitting on a bus. The Englishman gets up, presses the 'stop' button and only then realises it's the wrong place to get off. It doesn't matter *(δεν έχει σημασία/δεν πειράζει)*. Even if his actual stop is fifteen hours walk away and starving crocodiles are swimming outside in rivers of nuclear waste, Mr Smith will feel compelled to leave the bus. He pressed that button and he must get off. That's the agreement. In exactly the same situation, a true Greek would blast the driver for pulling in at the wrong stop. Total opposites.

A common view in Greece, and much of the world, is that the English are emotionally repressed and the Greeks fully liberated. Or do Greeks quickly learn that shouting avoids expressing real feelings and is the only way to get served in a bank? This cold Englishman *(Άγγλος/Εγγλέζος)* still hasn't made up his mind. The eternal chaos in Greece is both amusing and frustrating. A two-minute task in London can take two weeks in Athens, no joking, particularly where public services are involved. Cat Stevens, a Greek Cypriot, was inspired to write *Morning Has Broken* after joining an afternoon queue in Syntagma Post Office.

All the differences in the world don't mean we can't admire each other, putting aside the Elgin (Parthenon) Marbles held captive in the British Museum *(Βρετανικό Μουσείο)*. The English were impressed by the 30-day period of national mourning declared in Greece after a plane carrying EU grant application forms crashed - until we realised they were actually our forms. And the Greeks have always liked the English sense of humour *(αγγλικό χιούμορ)*. We've had a few wits in charge, it's true. Kennedy, upset by suggestions in the US press that Jackie was a heavy drinker, asked then premier Harold Macmillan how he would respond if British papers claimed his wife, Dorothy, was an alcoholic. 'Supermac' said he would tell reporters:

Έπρεπε να είχατε δει τη μάνα της
You should have seen her mother

I first thought of doing a lesson on England after coming across a reference in Greek to what I read as George Bernard So *(Σω)*. But it turns out that Mr So was in fact Irish. The first word, therefore, to learn when talking about the English, or at least about me, must be ignorant *(αμαθής)*, followed by arrogant *(αλαζόνας)* and let's never forget imperialist *(ιμπεριαλιστής)*.

One thing's for sure: England is everywhere *(παντού)* in Greece, especially Athens. It's simply not possible to escape. You have a much better chance in Glasgow. My street sign has an English translation - as do roads throughout Greece - and the corner store boasts Mr Men books in Greek! BHS and Marks & Spencer are here as well as Cadbury's chocolate and Earl Grey tea. English films play at my local cinema while TV shows the old Ealing comedies (mercifully undubbed by the tolerant Greeks who prefer subtitles) and has more coverage of Man. United games than in Manchester itself.

Half of all Greeks between 25 and 50 have visited or studied in England, be it London *(Λονδίνο)*, Liverpool *(Λίβερπουλ)* or my home town of High Wycombe *(Χαϊ Γουίκομ,* world copyright claimed). Advance 50 years and the Greeks might well speak as much English as Greek. Or more? Considering all this, is it still worth learning Greek? No. But do visit this intriguing country. For us pompous Anglos, the second greatest thing about Greece is its tremendous openness. Ring up a top hotel and the receptionist immediately says: 'I'll put you through.' Nothing wrong with that except I was calling world chess champion Garry Kasparov and I could have been anyone. I could have been a contender.

And the greatest? A few years ago, an Athens bus driver, worried his job was in danger under a new government, climbed on top of his bus and threatened to shoot himself unless the transport minister personally came and talked to him. Now important politicians can't just stop work and go and have a chat with suicidal bus drivers. For a start, there's far too many of them. You know what happened, don't you? The kind-hearted minister went along and promptly got his head blown off.

No of course he didn't. They talked (in his office). Crisis over. Life is often a challenge in Greece but it is rarely cheap.

WORDS I HAVE REPRESSED UNTO MYSELF

Λονδίνο	London
το αγγλικό χιούμορ	English sense of humour
Ουίνστον Τσώρτσιλ	Winston Churchill
ο Πύργος του Λονδίνου	Tower of London
Μπιγκ Μπεν	Big Ben
η Βουλή των Κοινοτήτων	House of Commons
Σαίξπηρ	Shakespeare
οι Μπητλς	The Beatles
το Πανεπιστήμιο της Οξφόρδης	University of Oxford
Χαϊ Γουίκομ	High Wycombe

LESSON 17

The Bible

Saint Matthew wrote a mighty fine Gospel but he wouldn't have made much of a journalist.

He had a problem with introductions you see. *Το κατά Ματθαίον Ευαγγέλιον* (The Gospel according to St Matthew) begins with a massive list of Jesus' ancestors which, in the hands of any competent sub-editor, would have automatically become 'The guy had a lot of relatives'.

Matthew had bigger things on his mind and clearly couldn't have kicked off with 'Hi, my name's Matt!' But, still, he should have got some professional advice. You can go too far. At the *Athens News* we'd whittled down a title for one hugely complicated story to *Psychotic pervert kills three sons in argument over last mint* before learning that the accused had passionately denied any involvement. Strongly believing that everyone is innocent till proven guilty, the title was immediately changed to *Psychotic pervert denies killing three sons in argument over last mint*. The subtitle stayed the same: *Tragedy as police find unopened box of tic tacs*.

I suspect Jesus would have shown compassion to that poor man. Maybe the Menthol Beast, our neutral nickname, would have been told to 'Go now - but suck no more'. As for Jesus' wise advice for dealing with adultery, if any Greeks had been on the spot we can safely assume that no stone - first, second or 567th - would have been thrown. They're a forgiving race.

There's no direct conversation on record between Jesus and a Greek which is a great shame because it would be fascinating to know Christ's views on cheese pies. If Greeks had formed his audience, the parables could have been very different. The stories of today's Greece - such as the armed robber who tied up a petrol station attendant and then served customers all night - would have shown equal creativity 2,000 years ago and influenced Jesus' teaching. There'd have been far more interruptions: 'There once was a man who joined a queue' - 'Was he drunk, Lord?'

Η Αποκάλυψη του Ιωάννου ('The Revelation of John') ends the New Testament and occurred on the distant Greek island of Patmos. The book mentions a series of signs and events which will tell believers the Second Coming is about to happen, such as an approaching ferry or a report in any Greek newspaper which includes the words: *Σε απάντηση, ο Τούρκος υπουργός είπε...* (In response, the Turkish minister said...).

One guy who did bump into the Greeks a lot was the apostle Paul *(Παύλος)* whose travels took in Corinth, Ephesus (now part of Turkey), Thessaloniki and Athens. His epistles form much of the New Testament *(Καινή Διαθήκη)*, the hit sequel to the Old Testament *(Παλαιά Διαθήκη)*. One of the most impressive things about the *Αγία Γραφή* (Holy Scriptures) is that they show you just how little the Greek language has changed through the centuries. If you compare the *koine* Greek used in the New Testament with today's demotic Greek, there is a considerable overlap. Hard then. Hard now.

That's not all. The Greeks of that time were uncannily like the Greeks of today; they tended to argue a bit and only reluctantly got up early. (I can rise at dawn, no problem, providing I go to bed at tea-time.) They also liked their food and wine. No offence intended but if any Greeks had been at the Last Supper, the Christian Church would now be celebrating Easter in October.

Easter! The highlight of the year in Greece and a more important occasion than Christmas in every sense, which some unfairly put down to a desire to save on presents. Everyone goes to church on Saturday night and then home for a special meal with friends. Ten years ago, in England, I was among the hordes of Hellenes at the back of the church catching up on gossip when there was a tannoy announcement appealing for quiet. It remains the only time I have scored a goal in church.

The climax of the Easter service, which moves many people, some of them offside, involves the whole church plunging into darkness ahead of a moment of high drama which never fails to make a big impression on all newcomers.

Before the explosion, or a splendid array of dazzling light if the other switch is pressed, people will have said to you *Καλή Ανάσταση* ('Good Resurrection'). After the service, it's *Χριστός ανέστη* (Christ has risen). Correct reply is *αληθώς ανέστη* (truly He has risen).

All said and done, God did well to choose the Jews rather than the Greeks. Otherwise, the first chapter of the Book of Genesis might have read slightly differently: 'On the sixth day God created the Greeks. On the seventh day He rested until being woken up by the Hellenes, angry they'd missed most of the weekend.'

GOD SO LOVED THE WORLD HE GAVE US ENGLISH

η Ορθόδοξη Εκκλησία	Orthodox Church
ο Πατριάρχης	Patriarch
ο Πάπας	Pope
αμήν	Amen
Ίντι Αμίν	Idi Amin
η Βίβλος	Bible
το Άγιο Πνεύμα	Holy Spirit/Ghost
η Θεία/Αγία Κοινωνία	Holy Communion
Ιησούς	Jesus
ο χριστιανισμός	Christianity

LESSON 18

An army of lips:
How to remember Greek words

Greek words tend to be rather long. Removal men in Athens use a crane when moving two objects - a grand piano and a Greek Scrabble board.

Size sometimes does matter and it's obvious that the length of Greek words, plus the sheer quantity of them, can put many people off. It's not only Greek. I know a diamond trader whose combination lock is *Novorossiysk*. Is he Russian? No, he doesn't want anyone opening his safe.

There are ways of getting around all this but first a story. Hundreds of years ago, people in England used to give directions by referring to the locations of gibbets. These were wooden posts from which people were publicly hanged for all sorts of offences, most of them trivial. Back home in High Wycombe, we're proud that not one visitor ever got lost between 44BC and 1989AD.

Today we need some linguistical gibbets, visual or oral trip-wires, to help us remember new words. The technique is used for other languages. Why not Greek? Try not to be too clever. Here's another tall tale. Do you have a bank cash card? If so, how did you memorise the number? Dimitris noticed his four digits, put together, formed the year in the thirteenth century when Eric XI was restored to the Swedish throne. Of course he soon forgot this. During an expensive Friday night date, the police caught him trying to break into the history section of the local library.

His mother says he should have just learnt 1-2-3-4.

No, children, let's not follow Dimitris to jail. That's not the way. The golden rule for remembering the golden rule for remembering the golden rule for remembering the golden rule for remembering Greek words is to repeat senselessly what you have learnt. Whilst briefly incarcerated, a son of popular singer Engelbert Humperdinck had his father's smash hit *(Please) Release Me* sung to him 50 times a day by other inmates. He has never forgotten it.

If repetition doesn't work for you, another solution another solution another (sorry) is on offer. Finding it hard to retain the Greek word for water? Plant in your brain the easily recallable thought it has something to do with a Roman emperor. Next time you want the word, go through all the famous Roman emperors you know and you'll surely stop at Nero and hence νερό (neh-RO = water).

Why would we single out Nero? Because our memory soaks up more than we realise. Deep within all of us there exists what psychologists call the *Cognitive Recognition Trigger* (CRT). Socrates is thought to have had two of these; Dan Quayle's was removed at birth. You might never recollect an exact word but your CRT can pick it out of a choice of 10, 100 or even 1,000. It's the same principle for an identity parade. Sometimes the CRT fails to work but don't forget that identity parades can select the wrong man except in High Wycombe where, to save paying volunteers, we make one guy - normally the suspect or his twin brother - walk in and out of the room 10 times. Only joking lads.

All this trigger talk sounds impressive and, guess what, it really is impressive, massively enlarging our memory capacity.

Where was I? Oh yes, we've done water but what about wine? I'm crazy about the stuff, really crazy. When I die, there'll be two wreaths at my funeral - one from my workmates and one from Cabernet Sauvignon. Think of a crazy mad loony crazy silly truly crazy madman crazily smashing wine bottles. This should be enough to take you to κρασί (cra-SEE = wine). Amazing.

In an earlier lesson, I think I taught you how to ask the time.

Forgotten the phrase? Let's put together a series of mental pictures. Imagine a boat on the water and a rower putting a cup of tea on one of his oars - a tea oar - which quickly leads us, or some of us, or me anyway, to τι ώρα είναι; (tea-ORA-E-neh = what time is it?). Okay, you have to memorise the last word.

Test yourself on χαρτομάντηλα (tissues - normally the small pack bought at a kiosk). There is simply no way I could ever hope to memorise this word. My brain is too small. And so is yours before you get all superior. Think of South Africa's Nelson Mandela, a regular reader of this column, who is a nice man with a good heart. Focus on that heart, the heart of Mandela, the heart-of-Mandela. Say it quickly - heartofmandela, hartof-mandela. Say it with confidence - HARTOMANDELA! And say it one more time - harto-MAN-dila! They'll understand.

One more. Want to know how to apologise in Greek? Easy. It's lips and lips and lips. Many, many lips. An army of lips. A lip army (li-PAR-may = λυπάμαι = I'm sorry). Trust me.

All this sounds very silly but, to be serious, there is method in this madness. Our minds, characters and personalities might be easily intimidated and defeated by unknown, invincible foreign languages but our imaginations are not. May the best chocolate pudding win.

DRUGS CAN DAMAGE YOUR LONG-TERM MEMORY

το μπάντζο	Jo attacked the barman...ban her from the pub...ban Jo...*banjo*
τι κάνεις;	Having a cup of tea while kneeling down to change a wheel...tea-car-knees...*how are you?*
η τρίχα	Laughing at a tree for growing a hair instead of an apple...tree-ha!...*hair*
ο φούρνος	Don't bake the bread! I said no, no, no and again no!...4 'no's...fournos...*oven/bakery*
αμέσως	Your room is a real mess...a messos...clear it up right now...*immediately*

LESSON 19

Once upon a time...

Andy Warhol's famous prediction that everyone will spend 15 minutes trying to pronounce *ωτορινολαρυγγολόγος* (ear, nose and throat specialist) has already come true.

Today, more people than ever before want to learn foreign languages, Greek included. Sadly, teach yourself manuals are often much too complicated and there is huge public demand for simplicity *(απλότητα)*. The answer? Kids' books. These offer clear and easy language which we can all remember and then use when talking to adults, even if 'I want an ice cream daddy' might not impress your Greek boss at first. You never know. He might want one as well.

In Enid Blyton's *Οι Μυστικοί Εφτά* (The Secret Seven) series, Gutenberg Publications, you can learn lots of helpful phrases:

Για στάσου	Hold on/Wait a minute
Δεν είναι και κακή ιδέα	It's not such a bad idea
Άσ' το γι' αύριο	Leave it for tomorrow

Give it a go! There is a real thrill to understanding even a tiny bit of a foreign language, not that I would know. The trick is to avoid looking up each and every word in a dictionary but to plough ahead, doing a chapter each session and trying to grasp the general meaning. Sure this can take time - especially if there's a drawing to colour in - and sometimes you accidentally make up your own story. I read one book thinking throughout it was about a plot to kidnap a nuclear scientist and dangle him off a Bolivian mountain during Ramadan to save a mining village in Switzerland. In fact, a horse had been stolen. I only found this out at the end when I looked up nuclear scientist (ie horse) in the dictionary.

Another approach is to get the book in its original language (if the author's not Greek and, of course, you know that language) and occasionally cross-check since translators are fairly loyal to the text. Roald Dahl's masterpieces translate really well.

The simplest books are for Greek 3-4 year-olds, ie foreigners who have been here for more than 24 months. *Πέτα, πουλάκι!* (Fly, little bird!) from Asteris Delithanasis Publications is ideal. On one page you have two words, *το μήλο*, with an enormous apple opposite. At the very least, it's a generous clue.

For those who like a bit more of a story line, look at Greek books for the 4-5 age group (foreigners here at least eight years). I strongly recommend *Το Σοκολατένιο Σπίτι* (Chocolate House) from Papadopoulos Publications which starts with the standard fairytale beginning: *Μια φορά κι έναν καιρό* (Once upon a time). I tried this in my local post office to complain about the slow service, namely *με συγχωρείτε, αλλά ήμουν εδώ μια φορά κι έναν καιρό* (excuse me but I was here once upon a time). Alas, there was no happy ending.

The superb Patakis Publications series of fairytales for Greek 5-6 year-olds (here over two decades) includes the educational *Ο Παπουτσωμένος Γάτος* (Puss in Boots). Without giving the ending away, the very last line of the story is:

Ο βασιλιάς έδωσε την κόρη του στο νεαρό για γυναίκα και ζήσαν ευτυχισμένοι μαζί με τον καλό μας γάτο

The king gave his daughter to be the young man's wife and they lived happily ever after with our good cat

All very useful for parents whose offspring are about to marry a prince or are thinking of employing a cat.

Comics can be a fun way to learn. *Batman Περιπέτειες*

('Batman Adventures', Marvel Comics) often blends Greek and English. Read the following dialogue and decide who's winning:

Whhoooossh! Τρέχα! Kkrraasshh! Grarrrrr! Arrrhh? Akk! Nnnnk!

Nnnnk is an irregular verb.

If you really can't stomach the idea of reading kids' books or comics, don't automatically jump to the Greek translation of Sir Stephen Runciman's *History of Byzantium*. I browse through a Greek newspaper each day on the bus, dreading a passenger asking me something and then looking baffled, along with the rest of the bus, as to why this lunatic is sitting there with a paper which he clearly can't read.

There are loads of good adult books around. Koan's *Το Μικρό Βιβλίο του Ζογκλέρ* (The Little Book of Juggling) has a fascinating chapter entitled *Ποιος ήταν ο πρώτος ζογκλέρ;* (Who was the first juggler?). Good question. I excitedly read the first sentence:

Κανείς δεν έχει την παραμικρή ιδέα
No one has the faintest idea

Greek's a bit like that.

YOU'RE NEVER TOO OLD TO BE LAUGHED AT

το μήλο	apple
ψιτ, ψιτ!	here puss, puss!
το άλογο	horse
ο πυρηνικός επιστήμονας	nuclear scientist
σσσστ!	shh!
μια φορά κι έναν καιρό	once upon a time
τρέχα!	run!
ο ωτορινολαρυγγολόγος	ear, nose and throat specialist
η γκαζόζα	fizzy drink
γαβ!	woof!

LESSON 20

Useful phrases

Perhaps the most common letter *(επιστολή/γράμμα)* I get from readers - ignoring any written in Greek which I obviously can't read - is a request for advice on how much of the Hellenic tongue really needs to be swallowed. Feeling your pain, here's a survival kit of 25 phrases which you're bound to hear or want to say whenever in Greece.

Taxis

1) *Ταξί!* (Taxi!) That's not very hard, is it? Notice the stress in Greek, unlike English, is on the last syllable (ta-KSI).

2) If you're unhappy with the route being taken by the driver: *Πότε θα ξαναγυρίσουμε στο δρόμο;* (When will we rejoin the road?).

3) The meter looks suspicious: *Έχετε διπλή ταρίφα. Πρέπει να έχετε μονή.* (You have tariff two. It should be tariff one.) In Athens, tariff two is from midnight until 5am and roughly doubles the normal fare. A convention of international tourism chiefs voted *Έχετε μονή ταρίφα. Πρέπει να έχετε διπλή* (You have tariff one. It should be tariff two) as the unlikeliest phrase to be uttered by a tourist in an Athens taxi.

4) *Δεν πληρώνω* (I'm not paying). See *Readers' letters from jail* (Lesson 12 Year 23). A *minority* of drivers will deliberately get lost (watch the signposts), pretend you gave them a 1,000 note rather than 5/10,000 (always hand over the exact amount if you can), claim the meter is broken (get out immediately) or engage in general crimes against humanity (take their number plate). In my

experience, rip-offs are more common with an electronic meter. But many drivers are helpful and a lot of fun. My favourite, on the way to the airport, stopped the cab and got out to urinate by the side of the road, with the meter still trickling away.

Numbers

5) *Τριακόσια* (300) is also *τρακόσ(ι)α* which can sound close to *τετρακόσια* (400). I bought a copy of the Greek Highway Code for 300 drachmas. The kiosk owner looked at the comic, then at me, and said: *Είσαι ο πρώτος φέτος* (You're the first this year).

Common sayings

6) *Χρόνια πολλά!* For a long time I thought this meant 'Many pollas' but apparently it's 'May you enjoy many years'. Used for birthdays, name days and the New Year (see Lesson 15).
7) *Χρόνια λίγα* ('Few years') is not recognised outside this book.
8) Someone sneezes. *Γείτσες!* or *Γειά σου/σας!* (Bless you!)
9) *Περαστικά!* (Get well soon!) There is no 'Get worse soon!'.
10) At a wedding (normally Saturday evening) to the blushing bride and giggling groom: *Να ζήσετε!* (May you have a long life!).
11) Same wedding, same couple but you don't like them: *Να ζήσετε στην Ουαλλία!* (May you live in Wales!).
12) *Συγχαρητήρια* (Congratulations) Similar to...
13) *Συλλυπητήρια* (Condolences) Be careful not to confuse the two.
14) *Πώς σε λένε;* (What's your name?) The literal translation, 'What do they call you?', can invite a much wider response.

In a bank

15) *Θα ήθελα να ανοίξω ένα λογαριασμό* (I'd like to open an account).
16) *Κάντε αυτό που λέω και κανείς δε θα πάθει τίποτα* (Do what I say and no one will get hurt). The publisher's lawyers are not very happy with this one, I can tell you.

Renting a flat

17) *Κοινόχρηστα* (block fees), *προκαταβολή* (deposit), *ενοίκιο* (rent).

Emergencies & eating out

18) *Βοήθεια!* (Help!)

19) *Φωτιά!* (Fire!)

20) At a doctor's: *Πονάει πολύ εδώ... κι εδώ... όχι εκεί* (It hurts a lot here...and here...not there).

21) For quick service. To waiter: *Πεινάμε πολύ* (We're very hungry).

22) *Εξυπηρετείστε;* (Are you being served?)

23) *Έχετε παραγγείλει;* (Have you ordered?)

Reconnecting your phone

24) At your OTE office, say *επανασύνδεση* (reconnection) or *έκοψαν το τηλέφωνο μου* (they cut my telephone off) whilst looking seriously unbalanced. Reconnections are quite cheap and sometimes the same day. There is no social stigma in being cut off but paying your bill on time can earn community disapproval.

A friend's just bought something

25) *Με γεια!* This means 'with health', ie enjoy it! But even in Greek different nationalities tend to say different things. Suppose a friend has just bought a hat *(ένα καπέλο)*. The English, if we like it, will say *ωραίο καπέλο* (nice hat). And if we don't like it, we'll say *πολύ ωραίο καπέλο* (very nice hat). The Greeks, in contrast, will immediately ask *πόσα;* (how much?), instantly followed by *αστειεύεσαι!* (you're kidding!) and a mass shaking of the head. Next comes unending repetition of the price, *έξι χιλιάδες!* (6,000!), *ΕΞΙ χιλιάδες!!*, *ΕΞΙ ΧΙΛΙΑΔΕΣ!!!!*, interspersed with *πω, πω, πω* (dear oh dear), calls to relatives to share the shock and amazement, followed by claims that a friend of a friend could have got 790 such hats for just five drachmas. This one-way conversation nearly always ends with the owner of the hat being asked: *Μπορείς να μου πάρεις ένα;* (Could you get me one?).

THERE'S ONLY ONE PHRASE I NEED TO KNOW

γεια μας! ....cheers!

LESSON 21

Bishop takes Aunty Gladys:
Improving your chess

Όχι στα ναρκωτικά. Ναι στο σκάκι.
No to drugs. Yes to chess.

If only. No country has ever had the guts to try out this inspired slogan from the Greek chess magazine *Γκάμπι* (Gambit). More's the pity. The Bronx murder rate would halve overnight if social workers started distributing chess sets instead of clean needles. Notorious neighbourhoods would suddenly reverberate to the sounds of 'check' *(σαχ/ρουά)* and 'would you like a draw?' *(Θέλετε μια ισοπαλία;)* rather than drive-by shootings and violent robberies.

Chess brings out the good and bad in everyone. On the board, as at work, we hate people so obviously worse than us doing so obviously better than us. One chess player *(σκακιστής)*, an ex-world champion, summed it up perfectly by shouting out: 'Why must I lose to this idiot?' No sport more closely reflects the unfolding stages of life itself. During the course of thousands of games, we attack and we win; we defend and we draw; we blunder and, finally my friend, we resign.

Feeling homesick, I once played a game in which every one of my 16 starting pieces carried the name of a friend or relative back in the UK. The queen's knight was Aunty Gladys and the king's rook answered to Rodney (see below). I won but it doesn't work all the time. Another player, after a nasty divorce, refused to ever take his queen out, except to pointlessly sacrifice her.

Melons, just checking you're still with me, and σκάκι are popular here. A great chess cafe *(Πανελλήνιο/Panellinio)* is near the corner of Mavromichalis and Solonos streets in the centre of Athens. Not so very long ago, Anatoly Karpov *(Ανατόλυ Κάρποβ)* popped in and asked for a game. Without belittling Greek chess, let's say the boy did alright.

If you prefer playing *alfresco* (I've heard he's not very good), there are outdoor chess boards along the Paleo Faliro coastal road and in the centre of Piraeus, complete with giant pieces. Loser has to pack the set away. The kings are especially heavy. On a miserably hot day, an elderly gentleman will happily agree a draw in a winning position rather than having to castle queenside.

Try to catch a (summer) game if you can. It's a treat to watch spectators protest about bad moves, angrily shouting λάθος (mistake) or μα γιατί; (but why?), followed by a mass board invasion to demonstrate their 'much better' combinations. With two real players and up to 100 self-proclaimed experts simultaneously fighting to move the same pieces around, the inevitable result, after all the fuss has died down, is that no one can remember the original position. Well over half the people involved have actually won.

Newspapers offer good coverage. Browsing the chess columns, you'll soon notice that the same openings are popular everywhere, principally the Ruy Lopez/Spanish *(Ισπανική)* and the Sicilian *(Σικελική)*. The Poisoned Pawn variation of the Sicilian Najdorf involves Black putting his most valuable piece deep in enemy territory and sometimes spending the rest of the game trying to get it out. One grandmaster compared this line to getting married.

Chess champions like Greece. Current number one Garry Kasparov *(Γκάρρυ Κασπάροβ)* has made Athens the operating base of his web site. Karpov visits occasionally - if the chess cafe is shut, this means he's just arrived. Bobby Fischer *(Μπόμπυ Φίσερ)*, who will presumably live for ever if God wants to stay unbeaten, enjoyed this part of the world but found Athens far too noisy. Back in 1968, the neurotic American genius changed hotels four times in a single week. This sounds bad but bear in mind Fischer once told some Trappist monks to shut up.

On to the pieces. Ίππος (άλογο) is a knight (horse) and αξιωμα-τικός, an officer outside the chess world, a bishop. Our diagonal buddies also reluctantly answer to τρελός (fool or madman). Βασίλισσα/ντάμα are both used for the queen, βασιλιάς is king, πιόνι pawn (and στρατιωτάκι - foot soldier) and πύργος castle or rook.

Ah, rooks! Rodney, a lovely man I used to play chess with, allegedly died a few years ago. All his games had the same tragic ending. At weekend tournaments, he'd come bounding along, bearing a big, beautiful smile and bursting to give you an unbiased match report: 'I had my opponent totally pinned down, Brian mate, my queen threatening everywhere, his king trapped, he couldn't do a thing. I was *killing* him.' Suddenly the smile would disappear: 'And then the bugger swiped my rook.'

Always his rook! Always a bugger! It might even be on his tombstone: 'Here lies a man whose rook was forever being swiped by an assortment of buggers.' If the Good Lord delays His Second Coming much longer, I dare say it's because He's mulling over which of Rod's rooks to swipe.

WORDS I DON'T REALLY HAVE TO LEARN

ο λευκός	white (player)
ο μαύρος	black (player)
θέλετε μια ισοπαλία;	would you like a draw?
θέλετε μια μπύρα;	would you like a beer?
πατ	stalemate
Πατ	author's eldest sister (Pat)
ματ	checkmate
τα ΜΑΤ	Greek riot police
το ροκέ	castling
το ροκφόρ	Roquefort (cheese)

LESSON 22

Block your ears Homer!

One neighbour, two 10-year-olds, three judges, four journalists and five public relations officers. I didn't understand anything. Except that they were all swearing.

There are many reasons why foreigners should know the naughtier side of Greek. First and foremost, there isn't really a 'less naughtier' side. Greek is and always has been a mischievous language - flexible, fun and stuffed with innuendo. It's useful as well to recognise when someone is merely using a worn-out phrase and essential to know when to back away in an argument, or what not to say whilst in one. The other day, a man in a nearby office was shouting and swearing, seemingly uncontrollably. Then he winked at me as I went past. The moral of this tale is that in Greece it's not always as bad as it sounds. True, I was naked at the time but my point still holds.

The problem is that many swear words are not in the dictionary. And you can't always trust your friends. In England, I heard of a foreign student who was taught supposedly polite phrases by irresponsible flat mates. His 'thank you very much' was quite the opposite and he came very close to being arrested at the checkout on his first trip to the supermarket. Asking for a carrier bag did not improve the situation.

Despite this cautionary tale, I asked Greek colleagues at the *Athens News* to give me examples of bad language. Within 15 minutes, no joking, I had received SEVENTY-SEVEN colourful suggestions, of which just over 76 were unprintable, including the Greek for 'drenched in semen' and 'I indulge in sexual intercourse with your mother (followed by blows)'. Many referred to specific parts of the human body and you can rule out classical allusions to Achilles' heel or Midas' ears. There had not been such excitement since I asked the same staff for their favourite verse from the Bible.

Readers generally offended by bad language should go no further. Seriously. That includes you Mum. Quotes are from colleagues' translations to their MVO (Most Valued Obscenity).

In offices and taxis across the country, *Mum put it down please*, everyone will have heard *γαμώτο!* (f*** it!) from the verb *γαμώ* (to f***), historically related to the noun *γάμος* (wedding). *Γαμώτο!* has been used so often that its shock value has dropped dramatically. Its most famous deployment came from athlete Voula Patoulidou. Having just won an Olympic gold medal in the 1992 Barcelona Games and using the word *ρε* for emphasis and familiarity (sort of 'eh!'), she said her victory was *για την Ελλάδα, ρε γαμώτο!* It gave the sensitive *Athens News* gang a real headache. The published translation, which got a lot of laughs and not one complaint, was 'For Greece, f*** it!'

Another phrase, *όχι, ρε γαμώτο!* is close to 'oh for f***'s sake!' when a problem has cropped up. There's the highly popular *άντε γαμήσου!* (f*** off!) and the slightly politer - though obviously we're splitting hairs here - *άντε πηδήξου!* ('go and get jumped' with no reference to the 110 metre hurdles intended).

One star word in the Greek language Hall of Shame is *μαλάκας* (wanker) which you will hear every minute of every hour of every day on every street in every town from every age group. Don't forget to drop the final 's' when addressing some- one directly, although grammatical consistency might well prove to be the very least of your concerns.

As with words in general, the context, tone of voice and per- son to whom you're speaking significantly affect the effect of swearing. Face to face with a friend, *έλα ρε μαλάκα!* (come off it you wanker!) is radically different from shouting out *μαλάκα!* to a driver who has just cut you up. Only a few can get away with both. *Μαλακία* ('masturbation') comes out much closer to bollocks: *Τι μαλακία είν' αυτή;* (What crap/rubbish is this?).

Ever so common is *πούστης*, an extremely vulgar word for homosexual, which can additionally apply to 'anybody thinking or acting in an indirect, sneaky way'. Also on offer from this delightful language of Homer, *τα έκανα σκατά* (I screwed up, literally 'I made it shit') and the magnificently dismissive *στ' αρχίδια μου* which misses out the verb and means 'I write it on my balls', ie 'I don't give a shit'. My mother likes this one.

Unless a native speaker - only joking Mum and I told you to stop reading - it's generally best to steer clear of all bad language, at least until we've finished this course. Who knows, as the years go by, some of today's filth might become tomorrow's poetry. Look back 100 or even 50 years in English and many words then considered shocking have become commonly used now and some laughably old-fashioned in the eyes and ears of the young. Have you ever heard a teenager say good grief, damn or bloody hell?

So keep a copy of this lesson for your grandchildren. They might wonder what all the fuck***, oops, f***ing fuss was about.

MORE WORDS I MUSTN'T SHOW MY MOTHER

άι στο διάολο/διάλο!	. . . .go to hell!
ευχαριστώ πολύ	. . . . . . .thank you very much
γαμώτο!	. . . . .oh I say! (polite translation)
δε δίνω δεκάρα!	. . . . . . .I don't give a damn!
άι να χαθείς!	. . . . .get lost!
σκάσε!	. . . . .shut up!
σκάστε!	. . . . .shut up! (formal)
μπα!	. . . . .why!, well, well!, no way!
μπα μπα	. . . . .black sheep
ω!	. . . . .oh!

LESSON 23

It's all boondocks to me

On holiday in Mykonos, the Reverend Martin Luther King, Jr, was deeply impressed by the politeness with which Greek police had just arrested a fellow diner: 'You have the right to finish your meal. If you do not have a dessert, one will be provided for you.'

As the cops left, King got up on a table and declared: *Έχω ένα κέϊκ* (I have a cake). He later modified the phrase for a lesser-known speech at the Lincoln Memorial in 1963.

From the Declaration of Independence to the Gettysburg Address, FDR's New Deal to JFK's New Frontier, and Neil Armstrong's 'Giant leap for mankind' to Bill Clinton's 'Kiss it', stirring language has helped generations of Americans face the future. But very few realise that King wasn't the only American to be inspired by Greece.

Teddy Roosevelt *(Τέντυ Ρούζβελτ)* gave this advice to US businessmen when dealing with Greeks: *Να μιλάτε σιγά αλλά να κρατάτε ένα μεγάλο λεξικό* (Talk softly but carry a big dictionary). An earnest Jimmy Carter *(Τζίμμυ Κάρτερ)*, after a speed flower arranging course in Santorini, urged his countrymen: *Να εμπιστεύεστε την προφορά σας - και ήρεμα με τις γλαδιόλες* (Have faith in your pronunciation - and go easy on the gladioli). Following an impromptu Greek lesson in Thessaloniki, George Bush *(Τζωρτζ Μπους)* promised the American people: *Διαβάστε τα χείλη μου: Όχι άλλοι χρόνοι!* (Read my lips: No new tenses!).

Of all American presidents, I see Richard Nixon *(Ρίτσαρντ Νίξον)* adapting the best to Greek politics. His foul mouth would not have upset people here as much as it did millions in the US, particularly in 1969 when newspaper reports of his first inaugural address were forced to use the phrase *Expletive deleted*. After his landslide re-election in 1972, the chairmen of all major television networks wrote to the president, politely asking him to 'affirm' rather than 'swear' that he would defend the Constitution and not to repeat his joke about bugging a whorehouse.

The man who beat Nixon in 1960, John F. Kennedy *(Τζων Φ. Κέννεντυ)*, would also have done well. Greeks appreciated his wise advice, in English, to *Ask not what your country can do for you but what the European Community can do for everyone!*

Athens boasts two squares (Halandri and Ekali) and 10 streets named in Kennedy's honour but there's no monument. *Η Αιώνια Φλόγα* (The Eternal Flame) graces JFK's grave at Arlington and Athens too wanted something in Kennedy's memory but with a Greek flavour. *Το Αιώνιο Σάντουιτς* (The Eternal Sandwich), with visitors taking a bite, was politely turned down by the Kennedy family. Actually, in death the Greeks nearly always strike a civilised balance - mourn, move on, remember, eat.

Four *Φραγκλίνου Ρούζβελτ* (Franklin Roosevelt) roads are in the Greek capital. Asked about the absence of FDR's middle name, Delano, a post office spokesman said it wouldn't fit on the sign. Only Harry S. Truman *(Χάρρυ Σ. Τρούμαν)* has a statue, which is occasionally defaced. Nothing yet for Bill Clinton *(Μπιλ Κλίντον)* or Al Gore *(Αλ Γκορ)*.

Besides a whopping dose of patriotism and a generous nature, ordinary Greeks and Americans have much else in common: Both want government to leave them alone and neither wish to be led by Michael Dukakis. On TV, any mention of international news means the weather's coming.

Not everything's '100% chipper' between the two. American English is lashed by purists, both Greek and British, for its alleged barbarism. Places like EYE-rack (ear-RARK), led by that

DICK-tayta (dick-TAY-ta) SA-dum (sa-DAM), and Gree-NAYDA (Gri-NAR-da) 'prove' their point. What, they inquire, do words like *deadhead* really mean? And would Marlon Brando have won an Oscar for his role in *On the boondocks*? Personally speaking, I find 'Hey guys!', 'Freeze, you son-of-a-gun' and 'Get real, man!' very friendly and informative.

The biggest difference, roads and hospitals aside, is that Greece is as wonderfully safe as the USA *(ΗΠΑ)* is hideously dangerous. In seven years of life here, I have yet to see a single fight (not counting the hundreds started by myself) and would always choose to walk in the most dangerous area of Athens in the middle of the night rather than the safest part of any American city in full daylight. My apologies in advance to relatives of travellers in Greece whose tortured bodies are found bearing my book opened at this bloodstained page.

It's true that sometimes Greeks don't understand Americans and that Americans often don't 'get' Greeks. Why? Well, it's just a guess but capitalist America's greatest belief has long been that THE CUSTOMER IS ALWAYS RIGHT. This can sit uncomfortably in laidback Greece which has never wavered from its sacred conviction that THE CUSTOMER CAN GET STUFFED.

O SAY, CAN YOU LEARN...

Τζωρτζ Ουάσιγκτον	George Washington
Αβραάμ Λίνκολν	Abraham Lincoln
Λάρρυ Κινγκ	Larry King
Το άγαλμα της ελευθερίας	Statue of Liberty
ο Λευκός Οίκος	White House
Μόνικα Λιουίνσκι	Monica Lewinsky
το κογκρέσο	Congress
οι Ηνωμένες Πολιτείες της Αμερικής	United States of America
η Διακήρυξη της Ανεξαρτησίας	Declaration of Independence
το CNN	CNN

LESSON 24

Days of the week

One of the hardest juggling tricks to master is called Mills' Mess. It demands an almost impossible coordination of swirling hands and a series of snap decisions, all of which must be right.

But the preparation for Mills' Mess can involve much simpler movements which teach you the different individual skills needed on that day of destiny. It's like Charles Manson preparing his followers for multiple murder by sending them out to steal an orange. Every little bit helps.

Applying the same logic in our lead-up to the formidably difficult 'The' (next lesson), I had planned to do something easy like learning the months of the year. Unfortunately, there's too many of them. Instead, *οι μέρες της εβδομάδας* (days of the week).

Now don't take this the wrong way. I don't mean to be condescending but, just in case you don't know them, here are the days of the week in English:

Monday Tuesday Wednesday Thursday Friday
Saturday Sunday

Monday *(η Δευτέρα)* has been immortalised in song by the Boomtown Rats. 'I Don't Like Mondays' *(Δε μ' αρέσουν οι Δευτέρες)* was the explanation given by a young American girl when asked by police why she had gone round randomly shooting people. She is now suing calendar manufacturers.

84

Ex-Rats lead singer Bob Geldof was so impressed with the crowd at his 1997 New Year's Day performance in Thessaloniki that he recorded a special version of the song, *Δε μ' αρέσουν οι Δευτέρες ούτε οι Τούρκοι, ιδιαιτέρως οι Τούρκοι* (I don't like Mondays or Turks, especially Turks).

Now here's a funny thing. The Greek for Monday is very close to the adjective *δεύτερος* (second) which sort of makes sense as Sunday offically kicks the week off. Monday, therefore, is the second day of the week, as shown in my tremendous guide if you start at the end first.

Tuesday *(η Τρίτη)* is the third day of the week and, yes, you're right, *τρίτος* means third. Greeks still consider Tuesday to be *the* unlucky day. It's similar to how much of the West looks on a Friday and I mean the 13th rather than fish. The fall of Constantinople *(Κωνσταντινούπολη,* today's Istanbul, tomorrow's High Wycombe) in 1453 happened on a Tuesday. The Wednesday *(η Τετάρτη)* immediately afterwards wasn't so great either as it happens but that's another story.

People born on the fourth day of the week *(τέταρτο* = quarter, *τέταρτος* = fourth) tend to be a little withdrawn and inhibited, possibly linked to early-closing hours on this day in many countries. I recall my politics professor asking his students: Why do lecturers not work on Wednesday afternoons? Answer: So as not to interfere with their weekend arrangements.

We arrive at Thursday *(η Πέμπτη)*, the most famous of its 52 annual appearances being Maundy Thursday. It's the fifth day of the week (don't be ashamed to look again) and *πέμπτος* means fifth as in this example from the world of basketball:

Η Αγγλία ήρθε πέμπτη στο 'Final Four'
England came fifth in the Final Four competition

My more astute readers will have noticed the feminine form of the adjective. My less astute readers will not.

Friday *(η Παρασκευή)* is the start of the blessed weekend

(το Σαββατοκύριακο). For some inexplicable reason, nearly all public sector strikes are on this day or Monday - or both.

Saturday *(το Σάββατο)* is the only neuter day of the week. The weird expression *το μήνα που δεν έχει Σάββατο* ('the month which does not have Saturday in it') is a longwinded way of saying 'never'.

As for Sunday *(η Κυριακή)* itself, this has obvious religious connections such as *Ο Κύριος* (the Lord), *κυριακάτικα* (Sunday's best, meaning clothes) and *κυνοτρόφος* (dog-fancier). Friends say my examples can quickly get quite weak. I think they're jealous.

If remembering these seven days is just too hard, there's a chance you might not need to refer to them by name. Greek has a lovely way of moving back and forth by using *χτες/χθες* (yesterday), *προχτές/προχθές* (the day before yesterday), *αύριο* (tomorrow) and *μεθαύριο* (the day after tomorrow). Together with *σήμερα* (today), these words manage to cover a period of five days.

And unbelievably there's even *αντιπροχθές* (the day before the day before yesterday, ie three days ago).

What a language.

WORDS I'LL FORGET BY TOMORROW

μέρα με τη μέρα	.day by day
δεν είναι η μέρα μου σήμερα	.it's (just) not my day today
η Τετάρτη	.Wednesday
ένα τέταρτο ζαμπόν	.quarter (of a kilo) of ham
Τρίτος Κόσμος	.Third World
η Μέρα της Κρίσεως	.Judgement Day
Μεγάλη Πέμπτη	.Maundy Thursday
Μεγάλη Παρασκευή	.Good Friday
οι κυριακάτικες εφημερίδες	.the Sunday papers
ο κυνοτρόφος	.dog-fancier

LESSON 25

The

'The' is incredibly hard.

The Greek 'the', that is. In English, 'the' is 'the'. It never changes. Singular is 'the'. *I saw the cat.* Plural is 'the'. *I saw the cats.* It can't be shortened. *I saw the cat.* It can't be lengthened. *I saw the cat.* It can't be amended by an act of parliament. *I saw the cat.* Unlike Greek, it doesn't matter where it comes in the sentence. *I saw the cat. The cat saw me.* It's always 'the'. There's even a group called 'The The'. In the course of time, English has spawned Chaucer, Shakespeare and 'the'. And the greatest of these is 'the'.

In Greek, you guessed it, 'the' changes all the time in contextual accordance with the case of the noun.

Beg your pardon?

I confess I've been dreading this lesson, finally forced to touch on the grammatical aspect of Greek, such as the different cases - and we're not talking nice leather ones. Defenders of the Hellenic habit lambast English for having millions of illogical exceptions to the rule, in stark contrast to Greek, a sublime work of timeless genius (with millions of rules). Some of these rules, concerning cases, we now unfortunately need to learn. I'll try to make it as reader-friendly as possible.

Once upon a time, in a land far, far away - locals called it Scotland - a beautiful princess went a-walking in the woods. Suddenly a young man appeared. 'Oh handsome prince', exclaimed she, 'are you *the* one for me?' The prince looked deep into her eyes and whispered: 'It all depends on how the noun is being used in the sentence. This is what we mean by the case.'

We've already noted that 'the' never changes in English. Now for the Greek. Spot the difference between πυροβόλησα τη γάτα (I shot the cat), where *τη γάτα* is in the accusative form, and *η γάτα πέθανε* (the cat died) where *η γάτα* is in the nominative (I think). In this instance the (feminine) noun hasn't changed.

Apologies for the distasteful examples. For months I used 'vacuum cleaner' as my standard illustration but then I got a really nasty letter from Hoover threatening to take me to the cleaner's.

If the noun is the subject of the verb, use the nominative case. To tell if the noun is the verb's subject, ask yourself: Is it the thing doing something, is it the active word? In the sentence *The policeman beat the prisoner senseless*, think about who was doing all the beating. If you decide it's the prisoner, join your local police force. If the noun is the verb's object - and believe me you'll know you're the object of the verb if someone kicks you in the balls - go for the accusative. In the nominative case, the form seen in dictionaries, 'the' is *o* for masculine nouns *(o ναυτικός,* the sailor), *η* for feminine nouns *(η πόρνη,* 'prostitute, tart, harlot, whore, tramp, hustler' - see Lesson 10) and *το* for neuter nouns *(το ντόμινο,* the domino).

Have a look at these two examples which an excellent BBC guide *(Greek Language and People)* uses to show the difference between the nominative and accusative. The names have been changed to protect the identity of my friends John Charles and Mary Hoskins:

O Πέτρος αγαπάει την Ελένη	Peter loves Helen
Την Ελένη αγαπάει o Πέτρος	Peter loves Helen

O Πέτρος, despite coming at the end of the second phrase, is still the subject of the verb. He is the one doing the loving. Of course you don't know this unless you recognise that *o Πέτρος* is in the nominative form, proving yet again that Greek is a very easy language to learn for people who have already learnt Greek.

Την Ελένη is accusative. I knew a Helen and she accused me of lots of things but let's not get sidetracked. It's far too complicated to explain all the accusative noun properties, especially when Helen actually loves Costas, so try to master the nominative and forget the rest. For the record only, I give the accusative singular 'the' below - the golden rule is that sometimes you need the extra 'n' and sometimes you don't. By the way, I don't know if it's accusative, genitive or provocative but when directly speaking to someone you drop the last 's' of their name - *Καληνύχτα Νίκο* (Good night Niko) rather than *Καληνύχτα Νίκος*. If they don't have an 's' to drop, you don't say good night.

And, sadly, we too must part. But not before some farewell tips to the very few of you still seriously interested in trying to begin an attempt at pretending to learn Greek. *First*, don't, whatever you do, read this book. *Second*, speak a bit of Greek every day; keep to this and you will learn the language. *Third*, NEVER EVER give up unless you're tired or there's a good film on the telly.

One final thought. To learn to juggle five balls, experts recommend trying to do seven because five then seem much easier. In other words, this could be the right time to take up Arabic.

THE, THE AND THE

o . . . . .nominative singular masculine definite article
η . . . . .nominative singular feminine definite article
το . . . . . . .nominative singular neuter definite article
οι . . . . . . .nominative plural masculine definite article
οι . . . . . . .nominative plural feminine definite article
oink . . . . .definite sound a masculine singular pig makes
τα . . . . . . .nominative plural neuter definite article
το(ν) . . . . .accusative singular masculine definite article
τη(ν) . . . . .accusative singular feminine definite article
το . . . . . . .accusative singular neuter definite article
το τέλος . . .the end

The Greek Alphabet

A α alfa
a in sandwich

B β vita
v in veal

Γ γ gama
g in ham, y in toffee

Δ δ thelta
th in this

E ε epsilon
e in egg

Z ζ zita
z in zebra

H η ita
ee in kiwi fruit

Θ θ thita
th in thistle

I ι iota
ee in beetroot

K κ kapa
k in quiche

Λ λ lamtha
l in jelly

M μ mi
m in meat

N ν ni
n in nanny goat

Ξ ξ ksi
ks in sacks

O o omikron
o in cod

Π π pi
p in pastry

P ρ ro
r in roll

Σ σ/ς sigma
s in sausage

T τ taf
t in turkey

Y υ ipsilon
ee in beef

Φ φ fi
f in fish

X χ chi
ch (loch), h (herring)

Ψ ψ psi
ps in turnips

Ω ω omega
o in more cod

Notes

(i)   Work out the order yourself.

(ii) Some letters combine to form different sounds such as ντ (d or nd/nt in the middle of a word), μπ (b or mb) or αι (e in met). See Lesson 2, which tells you to see this guide, for more information.

(iii) *Punctuation:* The full stop (.) and comma (,) are identical, in form and usage, for both languages. The English semi-colon (;) is the Greek question mark. The Greek semi-colon (·) is now employed less commonly than in English. The exclamation mark (!) has the same function in either tongue; when seen on Greek mountain traffic signs, it means the road is about to disappear.

Further Reading

Regular study of the books below will nourish the conceptual skills necessary for a successful mastery of modern Greek.

Knife Throwing: A Practical Guide
Harry K. McEvoy (Tuttle)

Three Times a Bride
Catherine Spencer (Harlequin)

Colloquial Basque
Alan R. King and Begotxu Olaizola Elordi (Routledge)

The Sorrows of Young Werther
Goethe (Penguin Classics)

Ἄλλη μια περιπέτεια για τους Μυστικούς Εφτά (Another adventure for the Secret Seven)
Enid Blyton (Gutenberg)

Unicycling: From Beginner to Expert
Sebastian Hoher (Butterfingers)

Greek in a Week
Hara Garoufalia-Middle (Hodder & Stoughton)

I Do, She Doesn't
or *Why I Came to Greece*

Why did I love her?
Because it was her.
Because it was me.
(Montaigne)

You do not easily forget the person for whom you held up a *train*.

There I was, at a small English station just outside the city of Southampton, reassuring an impatient guard: 'She's just coming'. But as by far the most beautiful girl I will ever see in my life came running across the bridge, the train left.

That was six years ago. This week *she* left. She's getting married next month.

What makes us fall or stay in love? A gorgeous, tumbling black mane, an irresistibly lovely laugh, that single rebellious eyelash which defiantly stands out at 45 degrees from all the others, just like her in *any* group? Or being the person you need to collapse beside when exhausted and want to wake up curled around when refreshed?

Her tennis summed her up, the chaotic ponytail bobbing up and down whilst she ran for that silly ball as if her life depended on it. The pride if she made the shot. The temper if she didn't, quickly replaced by smile No. 564.

Once I was bedridden with asthma. Couldn't breathe. Down came the doctor to the flat. My sole memory of the time he took to fix up the nebuliser was of this amazing Greek in the background peeping into his bag and even gently moving one or two things to see what was there. That unbelievable will to look and discover. She said I inspired people but forgot this was because she inspired me. Within two minutes of the doctor leaving, we were making love. They don't make nebulisers like that any more.

Here in Athens things went very badly, she having already split up before I came out but - and the only reason I came - constantly refusing to rule me out of her future life. She found someone else and I finally broke off all contact, which hurt her very deeply. As suitable punishment, I served six months in the Athens borough of Kareas, a place which I have loathed ever since. Through it all, I always believed that when nasty Mr Time forced her to 'settle down', I would be the only choice.

But in the end, the attraction of a peanut-juggling, loose-wire, freelancing, argumentative, disorganised, highly unstable, irresponsible, casual, uncompromising, poverty-stricken, scruffy, provocative, perennial student melted (for the life of me I can't think why) and she opted to grow up, join the real world and forget or remould earlier ambitions. Rejection because you are less loved than someone else is hard. But to lose out when you are still loved more than anyone is truly unbearable.

Even now, I foolishly hope that when she's out walking by a restless Cretan sea, tempting the sky to come down for a closer look, or at home, alone and thoughtful, teasing her guitar, 'B's will flash in her mind and a thunderbolt of change occur. But unlike me, and the only thing I came close to hating about her, she worshipped strength and never saw the fundamental courage of weakness. Once made, her decisions have never yet changed. Never.

The way out for me has been to work, difficult since she is in every pen I pick up, especially the happy colour ones. It is forever heartbreaking to be here in central Athens writing in the middle of the night - I have no home to go to - knowing her bed is just 15 minutes away. I have no doubt I could have 'won' her but I never wanted to and so never tried, for which I will now never forgive myself. She has genuine respect for her husband-to-be, a nice man with whom she will be comfortably satisfied for as long as she wants. I wish she hadn't invited me along all those horrible weeks as part of her sincere wish for the three of us to get to know and like each other. Why did I go? I guess, deep down, I was rather hoping to be Best Man.

I thought I - and I alone - could give her total freedom, inspire and forever interest this little girl and breathtakingly elegant woman all wrapped up in one, keep her young and fresh and a million things more. I was a million million times wrong or, the most appalling thought of all, a million million million times right.

My time in Greece is ebbing away. I came for her...and I leave for her.

This is a revised version of an article which first appeared in the Athens News on 1 April 1994. The marriage took place in May. To the great disappointment of many readers, Church opted to stay in Greece.

About the Author

Brian Church was born in High Wycombe, seven kilometres from Tylers Green, on 18 February 1965. Cards and presents are always welcome.

After reading politics at the University of Southampton, 100km from High Wycombe, he began a PhD in cabinet government, also at Southampton, in 1988. The same year he met a Cretan student and it was in 1991, whilst on holiday in Greece, that the young Englishman visited the old *Athens News* office to complain about a spelling mistake in the main headline (sic).

Shortly afterwards, Church ditched his dying doctorate and moved to Athens in January 1992, getting a job as a proofreader with the then title-challenged newspaper. In keeping with its unorthodox set-up, he was demoted to day editor in just a few months.

Late 1992, Church moved to *Naftiliaki*, a leading Greek shipping magazine. He returned to the *Athens News* after it was taken over by the Lambrakis Research Foundation. *Church on Sunday*, a satirical column internationally hailed as very unfunny, started life in October 1993 and is still somehow going today.

Entering a difficult stage of his life around Christmas 1996, with extradition proceedings drawing to a close, Church proposed a new column. *Learn Greek in 25 Years*, in his own words, would have 'the sole and noble mission of offending billions of lovers of Greek the world over'. It began in January 1997 and appears every Wednesday.

Brian Church lives in Athens. Alone.

About the Author's Mother

Myrtle Church was born in pre-war High Wycombe on 19 April. Her main hobbies are photography in High Wycombe, walking in High Wycombe and birdspotting in High Wycombe.

She lives in High Wycombe.

Her children live in Aretxabaleta (Mike), Athens (Brian), Coventry (Sue & Pat) and Wantage (Debbie).

She visits them a lot.

Brian Church
An Englishman in Greece

BY THE AUTHOR OF
Learn Greek
in 25 years

Always
The Best & Worst of Church on Sunday
on a Sunday

ATHENS NEWS